Jim Bradshaw

# LOUISIANA PURCHASE

## *A Pictorial Retrospective Celebrating Louisiana*

*Text by Jim Bradshaw*

Louisiana Purchase
1803 • 2003
BICENTENNIAL
www.LouisianaPurchase2003.com

*Presented by*

Copyright© 2002 • ISBN: 1-932129-26-X

Published by Pediment Publishing, a division of The Pediment Group, Inc.   www.pediment.com   Printed in Canada

*"Let the Land rejoice, for you have bought Louisiana for a song."*

– Gen. Horatio Gates to President Thomas Jefferson, July 18, 1803

## Louisiana – the state where it all began...

In 1803 the United States purchased 600 million acres of land called the Louisiana Territory from France for $15 million (an average of only four cents an acre!) – making the Louisiana Purchase the greatest real estate deal in history. With a stroke of a pen, a fledgling nation barely a generation old became one of the world's largest and most influential nations. The Purchase secured the future state of Louisiana, plus what today is the better part of 13 states between the Mississippi River and the Rocky Mountains.

## Two hundred years later...

The Bicentennial of the Louisiana Purchase – one of our nation's most significant historical events – is being celebrated statewide with activities and events to entertain, educate and inspire Louisiana citizens and visitors. Events of this magnitude don't happen often and they deserve a celebration. And when Louisiana has something to celebrate, we do it like nobody else in the world, with food, music, and the "gumbo" of our many cultures.

**The Gannett Louisiana Newspapers –** The Advertiser in Lafayette, The Town Talk in Alexandria, The Times in Shreveport, The News-Star in Monroe, and the Daily World in Opelousas – are proud to present this pictorial historical book to commemorate the bicentennial of the Louisiana Purchase. Each day our five daily newspapers cover two-thirds of the state of Louisiana, reaching more than 538,00 readers daily and more than 615,000 each Sunday. Most have been the news of record for their communities for more than a century.

| | |
|---|---|
| 1865 The Advertiser (Lafayette) | 1893 The News-Star (Monroe) |
| 1871 The Times (Shreveport) | 1939 Daily World (Opelousas) |
| 1883 The Town Talk (Alexandria) | |

Throughout those years, the Gannett Louisiana Newspapers have been privileged to witness history in the making and to report on the countless events and people that shape our community and our lives. We share some of those memories with you in this pictorial book, chronicling how our state has evolved. It certainly reinforces the notion that history happens every day and the Gannett Louisiana Newspapers are honored to be able to record the past and to bring a little bit of history to our readers each and every day. Join us in the celebration of the bicentennial of the Louisiana Purchase.

### Acknowledgments

The Gannett Louisiana Newspapers would like to thank the Louisiana Department of Culture, Recreation and Tourism and Lt. Gov. Kathleen Babineaux Blanco for their support and endorsement in producing this book. And we thank Pediment Publishing Company and Brad Fenison for sharing in our vision and making this book become a reality.

Special thanks and recognition also go to the following organizations: The Historic New Orleans Collection, New Orleans; Louisiana History Museum, Alexandria; Louisiana Office of Tourism, Baton Rouge; Louisiana State Archives, Baton Rouge; Louisiana State Museum, New Orleans; Lafayette Museum, Lafayette; Louis J. Perret, Clerk of Court, Lafayette Parish, Lafayette; McNeese State University Archives, Lake Charles; The National Archives; Newcomb Camera and Art Supply, Alexandria; Noel Memorial Library Archives, LSU in Shreveport; Northwestern State University, Natchitoches; Opelousas Museum and Interpretive Center, Opelousas; and Ouachita Parish Public Library, Special Archives Collection, Monroe for providing photographs and items seen throughout this book. Their assistance and the collection of photos they provided, along with the photos from each of our newspapers, visually recounts the past two centuries and much more – providing a glimpse into the life and times of Louisiana yesterday and today.

*Proceeds from the sale of this book will be used to fund the Gannett Louisiana Newspaper In Education program. NIE provides our state's educators with the most up-to-date teaching tool available for today's classrooms.*

Louisiana is poised to open its doors to national and international visitors interested in a closer look at the historic events that led up to the famous real estate transaction known as the Louisiana Purchase.

*Louisiana Purchase: A Pictorial Retrospective Celebrating Louisiana* will not only give our visitors an insider's view of how the purchase came about, but it will make history come alive for our school children across the state for many years to come.

Great care has been taken to provide seldom-seen graphics, photos, and maps that link the places and people with the evolution of our state's history from that period going forward.

The text and photos also provide readers with a statewide view of the rich culture of Louisiana–from Mardi Gras to our metropolitan skylines, one can feel the zest that our state is so well known for.

I want to express my appreciation to all of the professionals with the Gannett Louisiana Newspaper Group for publishing this book. They embraced the Louisiana Purchase Bicentennial as a project from the outset and have proven themselves to be great supporters of the state and the educational goals of our children.

*Kathleen B. Blanco*

— Lt. Gov. Kathleen Babineaux Blanco

# Louisiana Fast Facts and Trivia

**Capital:** Baton Rouge

**Population (est. 2001):** 4,495,642

**Entered the Union:** April 30, 1812 as the 18th state.

**Motto:** Union, justice, and confidence.

**Official state website:** www.state.la.us

**State symbols:** The state flower is the Magnolia, state tree is the Bald Cypress, state insect is the Honeybee, state dog is the Catahoula Leopard Dog, state gemstone is Agate, state fossil is Petrified Palmwood, and the state colors are gold, white, and blue.

**State songs:** "Give Me Louisiana" and "You Are My Sunshine".

**Nicknames:** Pelican State; Sportsman's Paradise; Creole State; Sugar State

**Origin of name:** In honor of King Louis XIV of France

**Land area:** 43,566 square miles (112,836 square kilometers)

**Geographic center:** In Avoyelles Parish, 3 miles southeast of Marksville

**Largest metro (2001 pop. est.):** New Orleans, 1,344,360

**State parks:** 17 (www.lastateparks.com)

**Historic sites:** 16

**Climate:** Semitropical

**Political Subdivisions:** 64 parishes (analogous to counties in other states)

**Pro sports:** New Orleans Saints (NFL) (www.neworleanssaints.com)

**Major Industries:** Manufacturing, minerals, petroleum products, fishing, tourism.

**Waterborne Commerce:** Louisiana's five deep water ports handle more than 457 million tons of U.S. waterborne commerce a year. Four of the eleven largest U.S. ports (in foreign commerce tonnage) are located in Louisiana. Trade is conducted with 191 countries around the world.

**Petroleum Refining:** Louisiana is the second largest refiner of petroleum in the U.S. Nineteen refineries produce lubricants and fuels, including 16.9 billion gallons (64 billion liters) of gasoline a year.

**Petrochemical Production:** Louisiana's petrochemical industry manufactures one-quarter of America's petrochemicals, including basic chemicals, plastics and fertilizers. Annual production by the nearly 100 petrochemical facilities is valued at more than $19.6 billion.

**Natural Resources:** Louisiana's natural resources include 11 percent of U.S. petroleum reserves and 19 percent of the country's reserves of natural gas. The largest producer of salt in America, the total value of all mineral production in the state is the second highest in the nation.

**Forest Resources:** Louisiana's mild climate and abundant rainfall give it one of the fastest tree-growing cycles in North America with 13.8 million acres of hardwood and softwood forests supporting a large pulp and paper industry.

**General Manufacturing:** Louisiana's general manufacturing sector includes maritime, military, barge and recreational vessel shipbuilding, light truck assembly, aerospace and aviation facilities, automobile equipment manufacturing, food processing and apparel manufacturing.

**Seafood Industry:** Louisiana's fishing industry is the second largest in America, accounting for 26 percent of all seafood landed in the country. Only Alaska's fishery is larger. The state's sports fishing on both inland and deep-sea waters is considered some of the best and most prolific in the U.S.

**Agriculture:** Louisiana is among the ten largest producers in the U.S. of cotton, sugar cane, yams, rice and pecan nuts. It also raises important quantities of soybeans, beef cattle, maize, strawberries and truck crops.

**Tourism:** The state's largest city, New Orleans, is considered one of the most interesting in America and annually hosts more than six million visitors. Elsewhere in the state, more than a hundred festivals are held each year, plus the historical tours, outdoor recreation, and casinos attract millions of visitors annually.

**Coastlines:** Because of its many bays and sounds, Louisiana has the longest coastline (15,000 miles) of any state and 41 percent of the nation's wetlands.

# CONTENTS

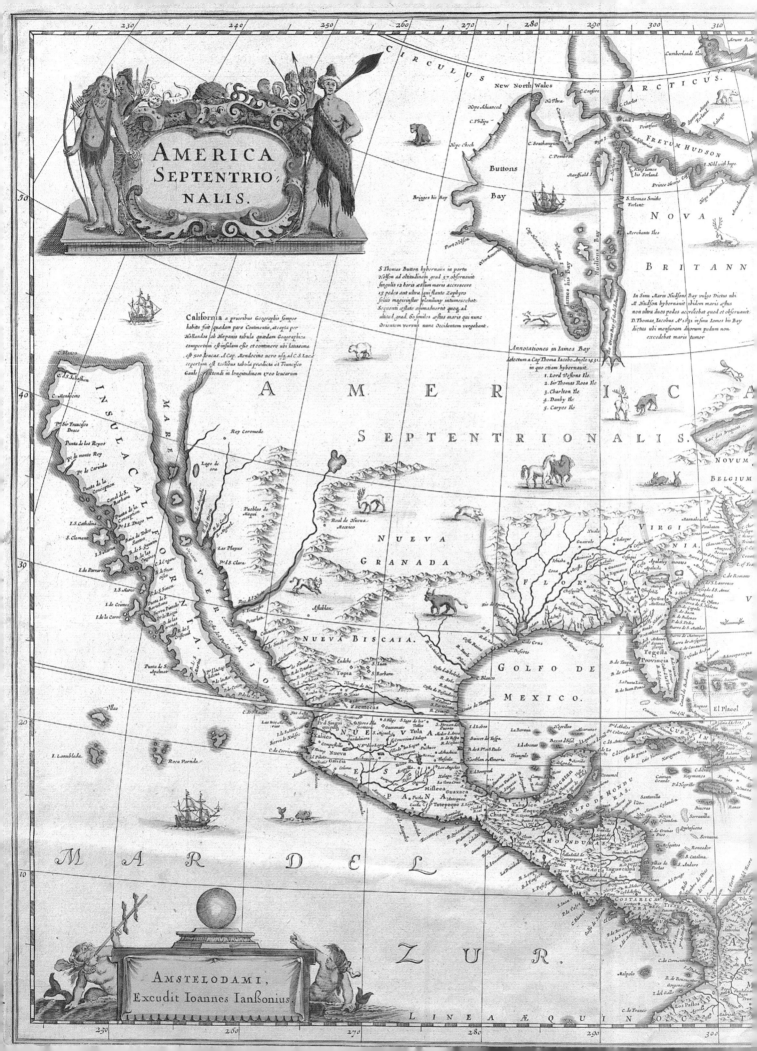

# AMERICA SEPTENTRIONALIS.

*Amstelodami,*
*Excudit Ioannes Ianssonius.*

## CHAPTER ONE

1682 - 1799

# Discovering Louisiana

*The first European to deliberately set out* to explore Louisiana was a Frenchman, Robert Cavelier de La Salle. He traveled the length of the Mississippi River in 1682 and claimed Louisiana for France. By then, the French were well established in Canada and the West Indies, and La Salle wanted to link those French possessions by establishing claims to the middle of the American continent.

As he saw it, with a colony on the Gulf of Mexico and control of the Mississippi River Valley, France could build a series of forts that would control the heartland of America. The river would give Canadian fur traders a warm-water port on the Gulf of Mexico when winter froze rivers and lakes in the North. In fact, there could be a series of trading posts stretching from New France, as Canada was then called, establishing a firm trading route down the Mississippi River to the Gulf of Mexico. These posts would also serve as a place where Native Americans of the heartland could be made friends and allies as France struggled, particularly with Great Britain, over which country would control the American continent.

On April 9, 1682, La Salle claimed the Mississippi River Valley and the areas drained by all of the rivers that ran into the Mississippi in the name of Louis XIV: "from the mouth of the great river St. Louis, on the eastern side, otherwise called Ohio, Alighin, Sipore, or Chiskagona, and this with the consent of the Chaonanons, Chikachas, and other people dwelling therein with whom we have made alliance, as also along the river Colbert, or Mississippi, and rivers which discharge themselves therein, and with the consent of the Montanties, Illinois, Mesigameus, Natches, Koroas, which are the most considerable nations dwelling therein, with whom we have made alliance … as far as its mouth at the sea of the Gulf of Mexico … and also the mouth of the river Palms, upon the assurance which we have received from all nations that we are the first Europeans who have descended or ascended the said river Colbert."

La Salle planted a cross and placed a Latin-inscribed lead plaque at the mouth of the Mississippi River, then went back up the river and on to France to ask permission to set up a colony at the river's mouth. He got his permission, and financial backing, and sailed again for Louisiana in 1684.

Unfortunately, no one on board knew how to get to the Mississippi River by way of the Gulf of Mexico. La Salle had come from Canada the first time, with Native Americans giving him instructions on how to find the river. There were no reliable guides in the Gulf. His ships missed the Mississippi's mouth and kept sailing west. He finally went ashore at Matagorda

*French explorer Robert Cavelier de La Salle*

Bay, near Corpus Christi, Texas, miles away from the land he had claimed for King Louis XIV. La Salle tried to establish a settlement there, but starvation and hostile Indians eventually claimed all of the settlers. La Salle himself was not around to see that. He was murdered by a band of would-be colonists who thought little of his leadership.

No white man returned intentionally to Louisiana for another five decades, which was just fine for the Native Americans who had been living on the land undisturbed, except for occasional fights with each other, for thousands of years. They came to Louisiana at first as nomads, perhaps 10,000 years ago, following the prehistoric animals that supplied them with food, fur, and sinew. By historic times, they had settled into six culturally distinct and important nations: Attakapas, Caddo, Tunica, Natchez, Muskhogean, and Chitimacha.

The Attakapas lived in southwest and south-central Louisiana and were probably the least developed of the Indian nations in Louisiana. They generally avoided Europeans, which didn't bother the Europeans, since the word "Attakapas" was commonly believed to mean "man-eaters," and Attakapas warriors were regarded as cannibals. By the time of European settlement, the Attakapas tribe had diminished to only a few thousand individuals in villages along the Vermilion, Mermentau, and Calcasieu Rivers in southern Louisiana.

The first European explorers to visit northwest Louisiana in 1700 found Caddo Indians who had lived in the area so long that they considered it their place of origin. They lived a settled existence in villages built on bluffs overlooking the Red River and its tributaries and were probably more advanced than any of the other Native American nations in Louisiana. The Caddo were apparently in contact with Plains and other Indian tribes and were the first of the Louisiana tribes to use horses. They lived in grass homes that looked much like beehives.

Tunica Indians lived in northeast Louisiana, with territory extending into what is today Arkansas and Mississippi. In 1706, after conflicts with the Chickasaw and Alibamu Indians, the Tunicas moved to lands held by the Houma tribe. Three years later, they turned on their hosts and killed many of them. The Tunicas were then attacked by the Natchez, who killed many Tunica. By the time of white settlement of the region, there were fewer than 1,000 Tunica left in Louisiana.

The Natchez, who lived in north-central Louisiana, were also highly developed, with a complex social structure. They followed a religion based upon a supreme being represented by the sun and had a great love of warfare. The Natchez people lived in homes built by timber held together by mortar made from moss and mud, much like the *bousillage* that would be adapted many years later by Acadian home builders in south Louisiana.

The warlike Natchez resisted European encroachment, and an early Natchez massacre of European settlers was one of the reasons that much of Louisiana outside of protected settlements such as New Orleans and Fort St. Jean (Natchitoches) remained unexplored and unsettled for many years.

Several branches of the Muskhogean nation lived to the south of the Natchez, the most prominent being the Houma and the Bayougoula. Most of the Muskhogean tribes lived east of the Mississippi River in what are now Mississippi and Alabama.

*Typical Acadian housing on display at LSU Rural Life Museum in Baton Rouge.*

Courtesy Louisiana Office of Tourism

The Chitimacha lived in southern Louisiana west of the Mississippi, with their major settlements along Bayou Plaquemine, Grand River, and Bayou Teche. Most of the Chitimacha lived near water and subsisted chiefly on fish and shellfish. They also planted crops such as corn and sweet potatoes, and very early on were noted by Europeans for their elaborate basketry.

The Coushatta Indians were not native to Louisiana. They lived in Georgia and Alabama and came to Louisiana in the late 1700s as Americans began to encroach upon their native lands. Neighboring Choctaw, Chickasaw, and Creek Indians lived outside what is now Louisiana but visited the state to hunt, and were also instrumental at various times as French, British, and, later, Americans intrigued against each other and sought allies among the Native Americans.

In some instances, these Native Americans welcomed commerce with Europeans. In most instances, they became reluctant allies, if they allied themselves at all. As historian Alexander De Conde points out:

"The Europeans came; they explored; they settled. They made good their claims to the land because they had the power to enforce them. ... As Tattooed Serpent, a war chief of the Natchez Indians put it, 'Why did the French come into our country? We did not go to seek them; they asked for land of us.'"

> "Why did the French come into our country? We did not go to seek them; they asked for land of us."
>
> — Tattooed Serpent, war chief of the Natchez Indians

The answer to Tattooed Serpent's question could be found in the French court, not in Louisiana.

As the 1600s came to a close, Louis Phéypeaux de Pontchartrain, and his son, Minister of Marine Jérôme Phéypeaux de Maurepas, became convinced that La Salle's ideas for settling Louisiana had been good ones, even if his execution of them was a bit off. By that time, Spain had set up a colony at Pensacola, and Great Britain's settlements were filling up along the

Atlantic seaboard. The French thought that they had better do something to maintain their claim to the Mississippi Valley, or they would surely lose it.

Pontchartrain and Maurepas were aided in their argument by French military thinkers who wanted a base on the coast of the Gulf of Mexico to help protect the French islands in the Caribbean, where fortunes were being amassed in sugar cultivation.

There was also the simple question of French pride: Spain and Great Britain had colonies in the region, France should have one, too.

King Louis XIV selected Pierre Le Moyne d'Iberville, scion of a powerful French Canadian family, to lead the settlement expedition to the Gulf Coast. Iberville selected his brother, Jean-Baptiste Le Moyne de Bienville, as second-in-command. The brothers sailed from France on September 24, 1698, and reached the French island of Saint-Domingue in December. Another ship joined him there, and, this time, to avoid La Salle's error, they sailed north to a point they knew to be well to the east of the Mississippi's mouth.

When they stopped at Mobile Bay, Iberville found an enchanting place, describing "sand as white as silver, over which rolled gently the blue wave of the Gulf." Behind the beach was "a curtain [of] tall pine trees, among which were seen majestic live-oaks and splendid magnolias, while birds of all colors chirped and sang incessantly among the boughs."

He decided that this would be a good place to stop while he searched for the mouth of the Mississippi. His colonists went ashore on Ship Island, near Biloxi, and set up a rude settlement there. The French had landed in "Louisiana" and were here to stay — although that was by no means a certain thing for many years to come.

In late February, Iberville and Bienville left Ship Island with about fifty men and began a systematic search for the river's mouth. They sailed for four days with adverse winds slowing their way and thick fogs obscuring the view. Then, a lucky storm drove them toward land and what Iberville at first thought to be rocks.

The "rocks" were actually driftwood covered with mud. The mud came from the Mississippi River. It was Mardi Gras Day, March 2, 1699, reason enough to celebrate.

Iberville was not sure at first that he had actually found the great river. This river did not look anything like he thought the Mississippi should. Nevertheless, he started upstream the next morning, eventually reaching an Indian town on the riverbank with "many cabins covered with palmetto leaves and a Maypole, without branches, reddened with several heads of fish and bears attached as a sacrifice." They named the village for the red stick, Bâton Rouge.

The Frenchmen continued upriver to Pointe Coupée (cutoff point) where the Mississippi was beginning to cut through one of its many loops and isolate what is now False River. Here, Iberville "used the neck of land, which is about a musket shot wide, as a portage for the canoes, sending the larger barges the long distance around."

After staying several days at a Houma village in today's West Feliciana Parish, the explorers began the return trip. At Bayou Manchac, which branches to the east from the Mississippi River south of Baton Rouge, Iberville and a small group of men split from the main

*French explorer, colonizer and merchant Pierre Le Moyne d'Iberville*

party and returned to Cat Island by way of Bayou Manchac, the Amite River, and Lakes Maurepas, Pontchartrain, and Borgne. Bienville and the main party continued down the river to its mouth. The brothers arrived back at Cat Island within hours of each other.

That journey convinced Iberville that he'd found the right river, and also that the land along its lower reaches was too low and muddy to establish a town. He built Fort Maurepas, the first settlement in "Louisiana," on the east side of Biloxi Bay in what is now the state of Mississippi.

When the work on the fort was well begun, Iberville sailed back to France for more supplies and settlers. Bienville, meanwhile, continued to explore the Mississippi River, looking for a suitable place to build a settlement. He found trouble instead.

As he was paddling down the river in a little canoe, he rounded a bend and — much to his surprise — came upon a twelve-gun British warship anchored near the riverbank. Its commander, Capt. Lewis Banks, told him that he had been sent to explore the Mississippi River and find a site for a British settlement on it.

*Statue of New Orleans founder Jean-Baptiste Le Moyne de Bienville, French Quarter, New Orleans.*

Courtesy Louisiana Office of Tourism

Bienville did what any resourceful explorer would do. He lied.

He told the British captain that he was not on the Mississippi River, that it was farther to the west, and that, furthermore, the river that he was on belonged to France and that a French fleet was just around the river bend, hidden by the trees. Bienville was convincing enough that the British captain pulled up anchor and sailed back to the Gulf.

Bienville named that particular river's bend Détour des Anglais, and it is known today as English Bend.

Nonetheless, the encounter served warning that the British were also interested in colonizing the Mississippi Valley. When Iberville returned from France in December 1699, he ordered his brother to build a fort on the first high ground he could find on the river, to protect against further incursion.

Bienville built Fort de la Boulaye, the first European establishment in what is now the state of Louisiana, on the east bank of the river about fifty miles from the Gulf.

It wasn't the best choice of sites. The fort flooded from time to time and no crops could be grown in the wet soil there. Mosquitoes loved the place; the Frenchmen thought considerably less of it. They stayed there only until 1707, although they maintained the soggy fort for emergency use until about 1720.

Meanwhile, the Frenchmen on Biloxi Bay were also finding their settlement not exactly to their liking. Iberville decided to relocate his colonial headquarters a few miles up the Mobile River from what is now the city of Mobile, Alabama. From there, he could keep one eye on the mouth of the Mississippi River and another upon the Spanish settlement at Pensacola. At that time, Spaniards were not very much interested in settling the interior of the continent; they were far too busy hauling silver and gold out of Mexico. But they were not enthused about a French settlement on the Gulf Coast that could be used as a base to attack the Spanish holdings during one of the wars that routinely pitted European nations against each other.

In fact, as Iberville settled himself into Mobile and began to make grand plans for forts and trading posts throughout the Mississippi Valley, the French government was diverted from its Louisiana colony by another war, called the War of Spanish Succession, which principally pitted the British and French against each other. Iberville left Louisiana to join the fight and would never return. He died of yellow fever in Havana in 1706, leaving Bienville in charge of the Louisiana colony. He had his work cut out for him.

While the war drained money, energy, and attention away from Louisiana, the little Louisiana settlement barely kept itself going. The colonists were able to keep body and soul together by trading with Native Americans, but they certainly didn't create any profits for the mother country. In fact, Louisiana became a drain on the French treasury to such a point that the Crown decided in 1712 that enough was enough.

For the next thirty years, the French government essentially gave the Louisiana colony to a succession of private companies, each of which promised to send settlers, rejuvenate the colony, and make profits for themselves and for the king.

The first of these entrepreneurs was Antoine Crozat, who tried for five years to do something with Louisiana. He fired Bienville as governor and sent his own man, Lamothe Cadillac, in 1713. But changing the direction of the Louisiana colony took more than a change of leadership. Crozat had been given the rights to Louisiana for fifteen years. He gave up after five.

One important event did take place during Cadillac's administration of Louisiana. In 1714, he sent Louis Juchereau Saint-Denis, one of the men who had come to Louisiana

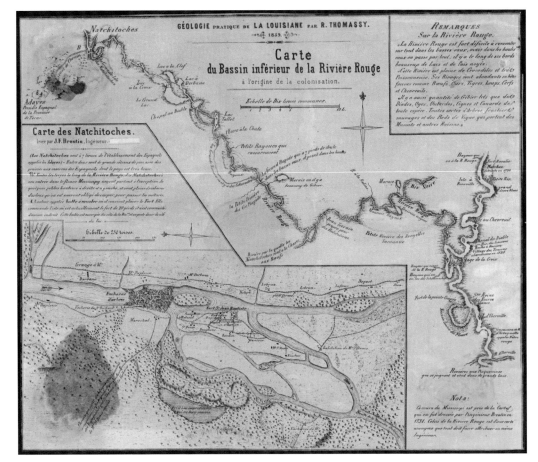

*Early map of the Natchitoches area.*

with Iberville on his second trip to the colony, to establish a military post on the Red River. Saint-Denis named his fort for St. Jean the Baptist, but, since it was located near the settlement of the Natchitoches branch of the Caddo nation, the community that developed around the fort was named for it. The city of Natchitoches in central Louisiana is the oldest permanent European settlement in what is now Louisiana.

About 1720, French military officers visited the area south of Natchitoches and established the Poste des Opélousas, named for a branch of the Attakapas tribe that lived in the area, at a place where two Indian trails converged. Opelousas became one of the few early settlements in Louisiana that was not on a body of navigable water. The settlement became a stopping point for travelers making the overland trek from Natchitoches to New Orleans and began to grow. By 1769, about 100 families were in the Opelousas area.

Cadillac was also responsible for the introduction of black slavery into a Louisiana colony that desperately needed laborers to clear and tend fields if agriculture was to flourish. African slaves had been introduced into the French sugar islands in the Caribbean many years before, so it was not a new idea to Cadillac. In fact, French planters in the West Indies resisted the idea of sending Africans to Louisiana, because they were afraid that it would limit the supply of slaves available to them.

*Bell tower at Fort St. Jean Baptiste State Historic Site, Natchitoches.*

Courtesy Louisiana Office of Tourism

Nonetheless, about 250 Africans were brought to Louisiana in 1716, and a steady stream followed for the next 100 years, sometimes legally, sometimes not. Most of them came directly from Africa, from Guinea, the Gold Coast, Senegal and Angola. A few were sent from the West Indies, most of these being unruly men who posed a threat to the Caribbean plantation economy.

The next to try to turn a profit in Louisiana after Crozat's failure was a remarkable Scotsman named John Law, who gathered backers and formed the Company of the West to run Louisiana. He sent Bienville back as governor and began to recruit settlers with some remarkable accounts of just what they might find in Louisiana — including precious metals, incredible medicines, rich soil and abundant wild game. He circulated his advertisement throughout France and also among Germans of the Rhineland and Palatinate areas of central Europe. Thousands of these would eventually come to Louisiana and settle on what became known as the "German Coast" on the west bank of the Mississippi River, or as it was called in French, Côte des Allemands. The St. Charles Parish town of Des Allemands derived its name from this "coast."

While Law sought settlers in Europe, Bienville was hard at work in Louisiana, building the settlement on the Mississippi River that would become the new capital of the colony. In early 1717, he sent a plan to Paris for the town that he hoped to build on a broad bend in the river that had captured his imagination on his first trip to that spot eighteen years before.

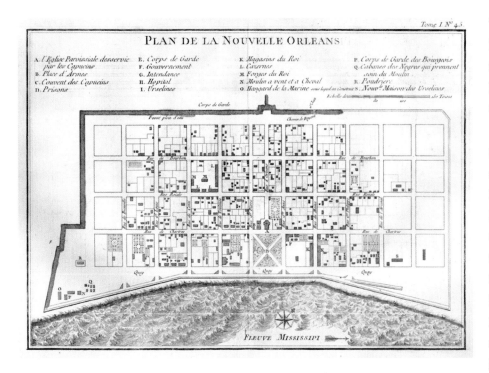

*The plan for New Orleans drawn up by Adrien de Pauger in 1720.*

The Company of the West liked the idea and suggested that the new town should be named for the Duke of Orléans.

France already had a town honoring the duke, called Orléans, so the Louisiana town became la Nouvelle Orléans — New Orleans. Fifty men went to the site in early 1718 and began to clear the trees and brush. In 1720, Adrien de Pauger, an engineer, was sent from France to make formal plans for the town and oversee its construction. He drew up a plan of streets stretching back from the river in a series of squares, with a large central plaza facing the river. The plaza today is called Jackson Square and his original little town has become New Orleans's famed French Quarter.

Law continued the importation of black slaves into Louisiana as well, so much so, that by 1724 there were nearly as many Africans as Europeans in the Louisiana colony, a fact that made the Europeans nervous. To make certain that the growing number of slaves was properly regulated, the colony adopted a Code Noir (Black Code), adapted from similar regulations in effect in Saint-Domingue. The code effectively banned Jews from the colony and established Catholicism as the only accepted religion in Louisiana, but its principal parts dealt with slaves and slavery in the colony.

It prohibited marriages between white and black people; mandated Catholic instruction for slaves; forbade slave work on Sundays and holidays; mandated that slave families were not to be broken up through sale; established basic rights to food, clothing, and housing for slaves; forbade Negroes to carry weapons; and provided penalties for slaves and slave masters who did not follow the rules.

With all of this town building and new blood, the little colony was beginning to show signs of progress by 1726, when Bienville was called back to France, principally for political reasons. He was replaced by Etienne de Périer, under whose eye the colony continued to show signs that it might finally realize its potential.

But then the money ran out.

The Louisiana colony was making progress, but not enough profit. The Natchez Indians rose up on November 28, 1729, and massacred 250 colonists, bringing on two years of warfare in which the belligerent Natchez were all but annihilated, but at an expense that the Company of the West could not bear. In 1731, the company gave the colony back to the French government, which sent Bienville back for his third term as Louisiana's governor — a term in which he had yet another run of bad luck.

Just as it appeared that Louisiana might grow enough food to support itself, a hurricane swept through lower Louisiana in 1740, wiping out crops that were vital to the colony.

In 1743, Bienville gave up for good and went back to France. He was replaced by Pierre Rigaud, Marquis de Vaudreuil, who governed until 1753. It was during his administration that cotton became a major crop in Louisiana, but, more important, that the Jesuit priests, in 1751, brought sugarcane from Saint-Domingue and began to plant it in Louisiana. Vaudreuil was replaced as governor in 1753 by Louis Billouart, Chevalier de Kerlerec, whose administration was hampered by another war between France and England, called the Seven Years' War in Europe and the French and Indian War in Louisiana. It is also quite possible that he was hampered by his view of the citizenry of the place. He reported just before leaving that Louisiana was in deplorable financial condition, and that the people who lived here were broke, lazy, and drank too much.

*The earlier settlers faced the challenges of swamplands like these.*

Courtesy Louisiana Office of Tourism

One of the effects of that war was to give the British control of a region of Canada that was then probably unknown to Louisiana at that time. It was called *Acadie,* the home of the Acadians. In 1755, the British decided that the Acadians could no longer stay there, and deported them by the thousands to British colonies along the Eastern seaboard, and a good number of them to prisons in England. At the end of the war, many of these Acadians would begin looking for a place where they could continue to be French, Catholic, and independent. They would come in later years by the thousands to settle in south Louisiana.

The British won the French and Indian War, which was formally ended by the Treaty of Paris of 1763. Under that treaty, Great Britain was given control of all French lands east of the Mississippi River with the exception of the Isle d'Orléans, the "Island of Orleans," and, because Spain had unfortunately allied itself with the losing French, the British also were given Spanish-held Florida.

The Treaty of 1763 was responsible also for the development in central Louisiana of the town that became Alexandria. A fort had been established after the founding of Natchitoches at Les Rapides — a portage on the Red River at Pineville, across the river from modern Alexandria— to protect the growing river commerce. Then, in the middle 1760s, a group of Appalachee Indians, who did not want to live under British rule after their land was ceded by the treaty, moved to Les Rapides. Capuchin priests built a chapel for them and, with church and fort, the seeds of settlement were sown. The first commandant of the Rapides post,

Etienne Maraffet Layssard, was appointed in 1770. In 1790, two traders, Alexander Fulton and William Miller, set up a business across the river from the Rapides outpost and began to acquire land around their trading post. Their land holdings eventually grew to thousands of acres that they resold to pioneers moving into the rich bottomlands along the river.

To compensate for the loss of Florida, the French, who were losing money in the colony anyway, gave New Orleans and all of Louisiana west of the Mississippi to Spain, but kept the deal secret from the people of Louisiana until the middle of 1764. When the Frenchmen in New Orleans heard about the transfer, they were not happy. They were even less happy when, on March 5, 1766, Antonio de Ulloa arrived in Louisiana to take control in the name of King Charles III of Spain.

Louisianians had lived under the flag of France for sixty-five years and considered themselves Frenchmen. They were shocked and upset when they were told that France had given their colony to Spain. For one thing, the colony had been loosely governed — if not neglected outright — by France, but Spain had the reputation of keeping a tight rein on her colonies. The people of Louisiana wanted less government, not more.

After a mass meeting in New Orleans, the Frenchmen sent wealthy businessman Jean Milhet to France to plead with King Louis XV to reconsider and keep Louisiana French. Milhet went first to Bienville, who was then an old man living in Paris, but who apparently had little influence in French government. When Bienville and Milhet went to plead with the king, he would not see them.

They were finally able to see Etienne-François Choiseul-Stainville, the prime minister, but he refused to even consider the idea of keeping Louisiana. When Milhet returned with the news of his reception, the people of New Orleans were first incredulous, then upset, then just plain angry. Ulloa's arrival did little to help things. When he reached New Orleans in March 1766, he brought only seventy-five men with him, which, in the words of one historian, was "just enough to make the people mad and not enough to control them."

*An aerial view of modern-era Alexandria, circa 1955.*

His first report to Spain was just as gloomy as Kerlerec's last report to France. Ulloa found that practically every public building needed major repairs. The church in New Orleans, he said, was in such bad shape that "it has been decided to remove the Holy Sacrament and place it in a guard house."

And, if the physical problems were not enough, the people just didn't like him.

As Louisiana State University historian Edwin Adams Davis describes him, "He was a small, thin man with an unpleasant voice, an almost unbearable forced laugh, suspicious eyes, and a hypocritical air and an excitable and nervous temperament. He was absent-minded and at times forgot his diplomatic and courtly manners with the proper-mannered French officials. His Catholic Majesty [King Charles III] could not have chosen a man worse fitted to inaugurate Spanish government in Louisiana."

To make matters worse, he immediately offended New Orleans society.

Shortly after his arrival, Ulloa married Francisa Ramierez de Laredo, who came to Louisiana from Peru. He met her at La Balise, a tiny outpost at the mouth of the Mississippi River and married her aboard a ship there. New Orleans society regarded this as a deliberate snub, and the French snubbed Ulloa and his new bride in return.

Matters came to a head in 1768, when Ulloa began to enforce an order from Madrid that Louisianians could no longer trade with the British (which they didn't mind that much), that any trade from France must first pass through Spanish ports (which was a burden, but tolerable), and that only Spanish wine could be imported into Louisiana (which was certainly not tolerable at all).

"Enough is enough," French New Orleans said. "We will bear trade hardships, we will suffer rude officials, but we will not give up our good Bordeaux for *le vin abominable de Catalogne.*"

A group of prominent New Orleanians, led by Denis-Nicholas Foucault and Nicholas Chauvin de la Frênière, organized a demonstration, and on October 28, led a drunken mob through the streets of New Orleans. Ulloa did not have enough men to contain the near-riot, so he and his wife and small child went aboard a Spanish ship anchored at the foot of Canal Street, where they thought they would be safe. The ship had enough cannons and men to keep the mob at bay, if it came to that.

There are several versions of what happened next, but according to one of them, a group of happy New Orleanians who had been celebrating a wedding took their merriment to the Canal Street wharf on the night of October 31–November 1 and cut the cables holding the ship to the dock.

Ulloa's ship began to drift down the Mississippi River, and he, taking the hint, kept going all the way to Cuba, never to return.

Instead, the Spanish government sent as his replacement Governor Alejandro O'Reilly, who arrived in New Orleans on August 17, 1769, and immediately showed that he meant business. He brought with him twenty-four Spanish ships carrying 2,000 soldiers, cavalry, and artillerymen — enough men and firepower that New Orleans could get as mad as it wanted, he would be able to control things. He required the people of New Orleans to take an oath of allegiance to Spain, and he rounded up the ringleaders of the revolt against Ulloa.

Their trial lasted three days, after which five of them were shot. New Orleans got the message.

Ironically, more French speakers arrived in Louisiana during the years of Spanish rule than during the years when France controlled the colony. These were the Acadians, who began to trickle into New Orleans when Ulloa was governor (and, to his credit, were treated decently), but who began to arrive in droves during the O'Reilly governorship, putting a strain upon his resources.

O'Reilly wrote on September 29, 1776, "The arrival of these people, together with those of the same nationality who are already here and with those who may come, is a source of great embarrassment for me, as it would be for any other ruler, because as soon as they arrive, we must spend money on them, give them what they need, and continue doing so until they have a way to support themselves, which requires at least two years. To settle them we must provide them with arms and ammunition, tools, etc. Widows and orphans have to be furnished everything, and all of them need a physician, medicines and food. In the first two years after their arrival, many fall sick and the number of deaths is large, as is the case now, and having no orders from His Majesty, we do not know what to do: On one hand, we are motivated by charity and obligation to hospitality, because if they are not helped, they will inevitably die; and, on the other, we are duty-bound not to use money for ends that are not authorized by royal decree, so we are uncertain about what course to take."

*Blacksmith artisan at Acadian style village in Lafayette shows visitors how life was in the early history of Louisiana.*

Courtesy Louisiana Office of Tourism

All told, about 1,000 Acadians came to Louisiana between 1757 and 1770, mostly after 1763, when the Treaty of Paris ended the French and Indian War and they were allowed to leave the Atlantic coast colonies where they had been relocated at the time of the dispersion. In 1785, another 2,500 Acadians were brought to Louisiana from France, where they had been sent after being held in Great Britain during the war. By 1790, more than 4,000 Acadians had come to Louisiana. Estimates vary, but there are probably 500,000 to 750,000 descendants of those Acadians in Louisiana and elsewhere in the United States today.

O'Reilly also made large land grants to settlers in the Rapides area and gave them supplies, cattle, and farm implements. The first settlers were heavily involved in raising cattle and O'Reilly wrote that "cattle were exported by the thousands." Also by the late 1700s some of the great cotton plantations were beginning to appear in that area.

In 1770, O'Reilly was replaced by Luis de Unzaga y Amézaga, who had arrived with O'Reilly and who had actually held the title of governor at that time, although O'Reilly exercised the power. By 1770, O'Reilly had firmly established Spanish rule and was ready to relinquish the power as well as the title to Unzaga, who for the next seven years worked to reconcile the Spanish government with the French citizenry. He began to include more of the Louisiana French in his government, helped to arrange marriages between young Spanish officers and the daughters of French families, and himself married Marie-Elisabeth

Saint-Maxent, the daughter of a wealthy and powerful New Orleans merchant, Gilbert Antoine Saint-Maxent.

His marriage endeared him to the social set, but an even more endearing trait was his ability to turn a blind eye to the regular black-market trade between French New Orleans and its neighboring British colonies, even though the cumbersome Spanish import laws were supposedly still in place.

During Unzaga's term, Bernardo de Gálvez, one of the men who would leave a lasting mark on Louisiana, arrived in the colony as a young military officer. As the son of Matías de Gálvez, viceroy of New Spain, as Mexico was called then, he had powerful family connections within the Spanish government. He also made powerful connections with the ruling class in Louisiana when he married Félicité Saint-Maxent, and thus became Governor Unzaga's brother-in-law.

*Bernardo de Gálvez became governor of Spanish-ruled Louisiana in 1777.*

Given his ties and his own record of achievement, it was expected and welcomed when Gálvez succeeded Unzaga as Louisiana governor in 1777, an auspicious time, since the American colonies had by then declared independence from Great Britain. Spain and Great Britain had been rivals in Europe for many years, and it was no secret that the Spanish government welcomed the American Revolution and stood ready to aid it when it could do so without being actually drawn into the conflict.

Spain helped the American cause with ammunition, medicine, and other supplies during the first years of the war, most of which was brought into America through New Orleans.

During the summer of 1779, Spain decided to take a more active role in the American Revolution, and the government authorized Gálvez to aid the American cause with military support, although Spain did not become a formal ally of the colonial government. Gálvez had been itching to get into the fight for months, and was ready when the orders came.

He overcame the British garrisons at Baton Rouge, Mobile, and Pensacola, and in that way protected the American colonial army from attack up the Mississippi or from the Gulf Coast. His army included not only Spanish soldiers, but also Native Americans from Louisiana, and a number of the relatively newly arrived Acadians, who had no love for the British who had expelled them from their native lands in Nova Scotia. Thus, many families with Acadian roots can claim membership in American revolutionary organizations because their French-speaking forebears fought with the Spanish against the British on behalf of the American cause.

When the Treaty of Paris of 1783 formally ended the American Revolution, Spain kept all of the Florida territory that had been conquered by Gálvez, and the Spanish government made it a part of the Louisiana territory. This addition to the original claims by La Salle and Iberville would become very much a matter of contention a few years later, at the time of the Louisiana Purchase.

His campaigns enhanced Gálvez's reputation with the Spanish government, and, although he continued to be governor of Louisiana in title, he spent much of his time elsewhere, leading Spanish armies in the Caribbean. Two men served terms as acting governor while he was gone. These were Pedro Piernas (1779–1782) and Esteban Miró (1782–1785).

In 1785, King Charles III appointed Gálvez as viceroy of New Spain (Mexico) and Miró became governor of Louisiana. After more than three-quarters of a century of settlement, there were only 25,000 people in all of Louisiana, 5,000 or more of them in New Orleans. Miró did not think that was enough to defend the place if the British or some other power decided to attack, nor was it enough manpower to make Louisiana prosper. He decided to push for more immigration into the colony, with some success.

In 1785, a military fort, the Poste du Ouachita, was established on the Ouachita River at the future site of Monroe with Jean-Baptiste Filhiol as commandant. Before that, the area had been the site of a trading post and Indian settlement known as Prairie des Canots. In 1790 it was renamed Fort Miró in honor of the governor.

There were settlers on the Ouachita River at least by 1750, and a few tiny settlements sprang up, but none of them were officially sanctioned settlements of the government. An old map that purports to represent French Louisiana in 1765 has "Poste de Washitas" written across the Ouachita Valley, but no single spot is indicated as a settlement or fort. But once a formal post was established, settlers began to put down roots throughout the Ouachita valley. In 1787, Filhiol brought in two Canadian families from Pointe Coupée. Joseph Pivoto, a migrant from Mobile, was there by 1789. Several settlers from the German Coast found their way to the Ouachita shortly after that.

A few years later, Spain granted almost a million acres northeast of the fort to Felipe Enrique Neri, who arrived in Spanish Louisiana in the spring of 1795, where he represented himself as a Dutch nobleman. During the next decade he received permission from the Spanish government to establish a colony in the Ouachita valley and engaged in several business ventures in Louisiana and Kentucky.

About the same time, a Frenchman who styled himself Joseph Marquis de Maison Rouge, was given 200,000 acres south of the fort.

Both the baron and the marquis promised to bring in settlers. Neither man lived up to his promise, and, despite their large holdings, neither actually had a great deal to do with the ultimate development of the area.

It was also during Miró's administration that the greatest number of Acadians came to Louisiana, many of them moving west of the Mississippi River and across the sprawling swamplands of the Atchafalaya River Basin to the Poste des Attakapas, as St. Martinville and the region around present-day Lafayette was then called.

Shortly after the Acadians moved into south Louisiana, Spanish-speaking émigrés from the Canary Islands, called Isleños, settled along Bayou Lafourche and below New Orleans, and another group of Spaniards from the region of Malaga in southern Spain, the Malagueños, settled on Bayou Teche at Nuevo Iberia, New Iberia today.

In 1786, Miró further extended Spanish hospitality with a policy that would provide big land grants to Anglo-Americans who wanted to move into Spanish Louisiana — provided that they (at least on paper) swore allegiance to Spain and adopted the Catholic religion. At that time, a significant number of English-speaking settlers moved into the Opelousas area and into what are today known as Louisiana's Florida Parishes (East

Baton Rouge, East and West Feliciana, Livingston, St. Helena, St, Tammany, Tangipahoa, Washington, and the eastern part of Ascension).

Yet another major wave of immigration began in 1791, Miró's last year as governor, when a bloody slave uprising drove thousands of people from Saint-Domingue in the Caribbean. Hundreds of white French planters fled to Louisiana at that time, bringing with them their black slaves. But perhaps even more significant were the thousands of *gens de couleur libres,* free people of color, many of them also slave owners, who came to Spanish Louisiana.

That migration not only reinforced the Frenchness of Louisiana's culture at a time when more and more Spanish influence was being felt, but also gave Louisiana the largest free black population in North America.

Baron Hector de Carondelet followed Miró as governor of Spanish Louisiana. Passions stirred by the French Revolution also stirred emotions among Louisianians who still hoped to one day become citizens of France again. The situation became critical in 1793, when revolutionaries took over the French government, beheading King Louis XVI, and, shortly after, France and Spain went to war against each other.

When clubs promoting "liberty, fraternity, and equality" — the proclaimed ideals of the French Revolution — were formed in New Orleans, Natchitoches, and elsewhere in Louisiana, Carondelet took a hard line against them. He forbade Louisianians to sing French revolutionary songs, suppressed pamphlets, and threatened to deport or discipline anyone promoting radical ideas in colonial Louisiana.

He told Louisianians that if they did not want to follow his rules, they could leave, "as the government does not care to admit or retain any subjects other than those who come to enjoy the peace, union, immunities, and advantages that form the basis of its prosperity."

A few folks left, most followed the rules, but by 1795, the flames of revolution were reigniting in Louisiana. The more outspoken of the rebellious leaders in New Orleans called Carondelet a *cochon de lait* (suckling pig) and promised him a date with the guillotine. Across the Louisiana region, people were in near revolt against the governor and the Spanish regime. Carondelet did two smart things in return.

First, he brought in more Spanish troops. If trouble started, he intended to finish it. But he also invited members of the French nobility who themselves were fleeing the guillotine to come to Louisiana. When these aristocrats found safe haven in Louisiana with their heads still on their shoulders, they had nothing but praise for the Spanish governor and joined with him in calming French Louisianians and steering them away from those who promoted an uprising here.

But, if Carondelet was able to suppress French sentiment in Louisiana, he and those who followed him for brief terms of office began to find themselves more and more entangled, or at odds, with the new American nation. As often as not, the tangles arose over questions about the use of the Mississippi River, the most important transportation artery in North America in days when practically everything moved by water.

As the calendar rolled from the 1700s into the 1800s, those issues would become the catalysts for one of the most important real estate transactions in the history of the world.

## CHAPTER TWO

1800 - 1815

# American Louisiana

*I*n 1800, the same year that Thomas Jefferson assumed the U.S. presidency, Napoléon Bonaparte made himself dictator of France and assumed the title First Consul. The two men had little in common, yet their actions changed the destiny of Louisiana, of the United States, and, quite possibly, of France.

For a while, it looked like they would become adversaries. Relations between the United States and France were peaceful enough — France had been a powerful ally during the American Revolution, and Jefferson remembered that. But then Napoléon's ambitious eye began to focus on America and threaten the interests of the United States.

Napoléon wanted to use the Louisiana Territory as the basis for a huge American empire. Spain held Louisiana when he first began to dream his grandiose dreams, but that didn't bother Napoléon. He was at the top of his military game and could get anything he needed from Spain. It didn't hurt that Spain and the United States were already at each other's throats, and that the Spanish government was already beginning to think that it may have to get rid of at least part of the territory.

At issue was control of the Mississippi River.

In the late 1700s, as more and more Americans pushed across the Appalachian mountains and toward the Mississippi River, friction began to develop among the farmers of Kentucky, Tennessee, and the Ohio Valley with the Spanish officials who controlled the busy port of New Orleans, and thus, the mouth of the Mississippi River.

Spanish officials at New Orleans regarded the river as theirs to control. Americans upriver began to believe that they had a "natural right" to use the river to ship their products to market. Spain challenged that assumption in 1784, closing the lower Mississippi River to all but Spanish commerce.

The American reaction was immediate, loud, angry, and threatening. Men from Kentucky and Tennessee threatened to use their vaunted long rifles to reopen the river. President Jefferson sent diplomat Thomas Pinckney to negotiate with the Spanish

*Thomas Jefferson*

**Opposite page:**
*Oil painting "Raising of the American Flag: The Louisiana Purchase Transfer Ceremonies" by Bror Thure de Thulstrup, circa 1903.*
Courtesy Louisiana State Museum.
Loan of the Louisiana Historical Society

government and, in 1795, the two nations signed the Treaty of San Lorenzo, which gave the United States unlimited navigation of the Mississippi and the "right of deposit" — the right to unload goods tax-free — at New Orleans for three years.

Most people thought that settled the question.

But the pushy Americans continued to grate on Spanish nerves and, in 1799, despite the treaty, tensions between American settlers and the Spanish in New Orleans became so high that Juan Ventura Morales, Spain's highest ranking officer in Louisiana, shut off the right of deposit at New Orleans. That meant that American crops sent downriver to market would have to sell quickly or rot.

Once again, Kentucky and Tennessee flatboatmen threatened to invade New Orleans, and American diplomats rushed to the Spanish court to protest what Morales had done. The king reinstated the deposit rights in 1800, but that did little to ease problems in Louisiana.

Both sides were preparing for a showdown. Spain began building up troops in New Orleans and the American frontiersmen began to store away guns and gunpowder.

President Jefferson preached calm. He appointed Robert Livingston as U.S. minister to Spain and told him to buy New Orleans and the area around it, so that the United States would control the river. But Livingston encountered a small problem when he got to Spain. He found that Louisiana was no longer Spain's to sell. On October 1, 1800, King Charles IV of Spain had given all of Louisiana back to France in exchange for Napoléon's promise to create a kingdom in Italy for Charles's son-in-law, the Duke of Parma.

Napoléon kept the exchange a secret, because he didn't want to alert other nations to his grand designs for the American continent. France and England were at war (as usual) at the time, and Napoléon was not in a position to keep British ships away from New Orleans. If the British found out before Napoléon could act to reinforce the place, they could simply sail up the Mississippi and take control of the city and, in so doing, command of the river.

The first inkling of the secret treaty reached Washington in May of 1801. Rufus King, the American minister to Great Britain heard a rumor about the transfer and passed it on to President Jefferson. The president didn't believe it at first, or maybe he just did not want to believe it. If it was true that France had taken control of Louisiana, it meant trouble.

"There is on the globe one single spot, the possessor of which is our natural and habitual enemy. It is New Orleans..."

— Thomas Jefferson

The Louisiana territory in the hands of a declining Spain meant one thing — there was little real likelihood of a confrontation with a Spanish government that was too poor and too weak to do much confronting. But it was something else to have Louisiana in the hands of the ambitious Napoléon Bonaparte, whose grand designs would likely be aided and abetted by French Creoles in New Orleans, who would love nothing better than to be tied again with their old country and to see France once again with a strong presence in North America.

On April 18, 1802, after President Jefferson became convinced that France did indeed have eyes on New Orleans and all of the huge Louisiana territory, he wrote to Livingston, "There is on the globe one single spot, the possessor of which is our natural and habitual enemy. It is New Orleans, through which the produce of three-eighths of our territory must pass to market and from its fertility it will ere long yield more than half of our whole produce and contain more than half our inhabitants.

"France, placing herself in that door, assumes to us the attitude of defiance. Spain might have retained it quietly for years. Her pacific dispositions, her feeble state, would induce her to increase our facilities there, so that her possession of the place would be hardly felt by us, and it would not, perhaps, be very long before some circumstance which might arise which might make the cession of it to us the price of something of more worth to her.

"Not so can it ever be in the hands of France; the impetuosity of her temper, the energy and restlessness of her character, placed in a point of eternal friction with us, and our character, which, though quiet and loving peace and pursuit of wealth … render it impossible that France and the United States can continue long friends when they meet in so irritable a position."

He told Livingston to talk to French officials and see if they would be willing to sell the New Orleans region, offering the same deal that he thought he would offer to Spain.

At first Napoléon said, "No deal." But by the spring of 1803 it became apparent that his fight with Great Britain was about to command more of his men, money, and attention than he had anticipated. And he came to realize that as soon as he claimed Louisiana, Great Britain would probably attack there and probably take it from him.

Even if he held Louisiana against the British, he reasoned further, it was still only a matter of time before the territory would be overrun by Americans pushing over the mountains from the east and settling in the Mississippi River Valley. He decided to make a surprising offer.

François Barbe-Marbois, the French minister who had been discussing the possible purchase of the Isle d'Orléans with the American Livingston, described in his memoirs what happened when Napoléon came to the realization that he could no longer keep Louisiana.

*Early nineteenth-century painting of Napoléon Bonaparte crossing the Alps.*
Courtesy Louisiana State Museum

"On the 10th of April, 1803, Easter Sunday, after having given his time to the solemnity of the day, and to the demands of ceremony, [Napoléon called in his counselors] and, speaking to them with that vehemence and passion with which he was especially carried away in political affairs, said, 'I know the whole value of Louisiana, and I have a wish to repair the fault of the French negotiator who abandoned it in 1763. … The English have successively taken from France … Canada, Isle Royal, Newfoundland, Nova Scotia, the richest parts of Asia. They are at work to agitate Saint-Domingue. They shall not have the Mississippi, which they covet.

*Engraving of Robert R. Livingston, by H. B. Hall.*
Courtesy Louisiana State Museum

"'Louisiana is nothing in comparison with their acquisitions throughout the globe; and yet the jealousy which the return of this colony under French dominion causes them proves to me that they desire to get possession of it, and that it is thus that they will commence war. They have twenty vessels in the Gulf of Mexico. … The conquest of Louisiana would be easy, if they only took the trouble of making a descent there. I have not a moment to lose in putting it out of their reach.

"'I think of ceding it to the United States. I can scarcely say that I cede it to them for it is not yet in our possession. If I leave ever so little time to our enemies, I shall only transmit an empty title to [the United States] whose friendship I seek. They only ask of me one town in Louisiana; but I already consider the colony as entirely lost, and it appears to me that in the hands of this growing republic, it will be more useful to the policy and even to the commerce of France than if I attempt to retain it.'"

And, Napoléon said, there was one more thing to consider, "I require money to make war on [Great Britain] the richest nation in the world."

*Crayon drawing of François Barbe-Marbois, artist unknown.*
Courtesy Louisiana State Museum

He told Barbe-Marbois he wanted 50 million francs for all of the Louisiana territory — the vast watershed of the Mississippi River and its tributaries that La Salle had claimed so many years before. Barbe-Marbois offered the territory to Livingston for twice what Napoléon wanted. He said the selling price was 100 million francs.

Livingston didn't know what to do. He had been authorized to spend a lot less money for a much smaller piece of land. It took weeks, sometimes months, for letters to cross the Atlantic and for a reply to get back. And Napoléon, now that his mind was made up, wanted a quick answer.

Two days after the offer had been made, James Monroe arrived in Paris to help Livingston with, he thought, the negotiations for the Isle d'Orléans. When Livingston told him what Napoléon had offered, the two of them decided to go ahead and make the deal, even though it far exceeded their authority. They did haggle a bit over the price of the purchase, finally settling at a total of 80 million francs, partly in direct payment to France and partly in assumption by the United States of some French debt. That price came to $15 million in American money, just about four cents an acre for the huge Louisiana territory.

*Engraving of James Monroe, 1861, by Johnson, Fry, & Co.*
Courtesy Louisiana State Museum

There was one problem: Nobody knew just how huge the Louisiana territory actually was. Neither France nor Spain had ever been completely clear on just what the boundaries of the territory were, so the U.S. negotiators did not know exactly what they were buying. At an after-the-sale toast, Livingston asked Charles-Maurice de Talleyrand-Périgord, the French foreign minister, just what the Louisiana boundaries were. The minister replied, "You have made a noble bargain for yourselves, and I suppose you will make the most of it." In effect, he said, "Louisiana" was about as big as the United States had the gumption to make it.

Indeed, it was a noble bargain. The lands acquired stretched from the Mississippi River to the Rocky Mountains and from the Gulf of Mexico to the Canadian border. The Louisiana Purchase nearly doubled the size of the United States, making it one of the largest nations in the world. Thirteen states were eventually carved from the territory: Louisiana, Arkansas, Missouri, Iowa, North Dakota, South Dakota, Nebraska, Kansas, Wyoming, Minnesota, Oklahoma, Colorado, and Montana.

News of the Purchase reached the United States on July 3, 1803, and was generally well received by everyone except President Jefferson's staunchest political opponents. The Senate quickly ratified the Purchase, the House just as quickly approved the funding for it, and diplomatic and military preparations began for the formal transfer of the property to the United States.

On November 30, 1803, the Spanish officials in New Orleans formally handed over the colony to France, in keeping with the secret treaty between those two countries. Twenty days later, the flag of France came down to be replaced by the Stars and Stripes.

Historian Rufus Blanchard described the scene in his history of the Purchase:

"When the change of flags came, the United States flag was raised, while at the same instant the French flag was lowered; and when they met midway, both were kept stationary for a few instants, while the artillery and trumpets celebrated the union to emblematize the harmony between the two nations as the one resigned its authority and the other assumed its authority over the Province of Louisiana.

"Next, the flag of the United States rose to its full height. The Americans shouted with joy; the colors of the French Republic were lowered and received into the arms of the French, who guarded them, while their regrets were openly expressed. To render a last token of homage to their flag, the French sergeant-major wrapped it around his body as a scarf and, ornate with its many folds, traversed the principal streets of [New Orleans] till he came to the house of the French commissioner. A troop of French patriots accompanied him

and were saluted in passing before the American lines, who presented arms to them as a token of respect."

The French and Americans were happy about the transfer. Napoléon, though having to give up his plans for an American empire, had the money he needed to try to continue to expand the one he was building in Europe. The young United States, once hemmed in behind the Appalachian Mountains in the east, then stymied by the Mississippi River in its heartland, had just jumped in territory all the way to the Rocky Mountains. And, standing on top of them, it was not unreal for Americans to begin to imagine what it would be like to extend their reach to the Pacific Ocean.

But Spain was far from happy. The Spanish also saw what the Americans saw from atop the Rocky Mountains, and realized that American expansion could only come at the expense of New Spain.

Don Carlos María Martínez de Yrujo, the Spanish minister to the United States, at first refused to accept the sale of Louisiana to the Americans. He argued that France had no right to sell it because it had not been formally returned to France at the time the sale was made.

When nobody listened to his arguments, he wrote to Sebastián de Casa Calvo, the former military governor who was still in New Orleans, that he should be prepared to fight the Americans for Louisiana. Yrujo even drafted a plan of defense for Casa Calvo to follow.

But, when the Americans began building up military forces in Kentucky, Tennessee, and Mississippi, even the militant Yrujo had to think again. He changed his tactic from trying to save all of Louisiana for Spain to making certain that the definition of "Louisiana" included as little Spanish land as possible.

He knew, just as Talleyrand had intimated to Livingston, that the boundaries could be disputed, and that the United States wanted as much as it could get. American diplomats negotiating with Spain after the sale claimed that Louisiana extended all the way to the Rio Grande, and included most of what is now the state of Texas. Spain argued that the Mermentau River, was the proper border, and that the Purchase not only did not include any of Texas, it did not include part of what is now southwestern Louisiana.

Spanish and American negotiators, and President Jefferson himself, searched out old maps and other documents that would support their positions and haggled over conference tables in Washington and Madrid. And while the diplomats argued, the soldiers took to the field.

Many months after the Purchase, nothing had been resolved and tensions were already running high when a series of incidents brought things very close to actual fighting. At first, plain old thieves — Spanish and American — took advantage of the lack of authority in the "no man's land" to rob one or the other. In a more serious incident, Americans and Spanish soldiers faced off after Spain removed an American flag flying over a Caddo Indian village in northwest Louisiana — claiming the village had been under Spanish jurisdiction for many years.

Louisianians were also bothered by the same thing that brought about another conflict some sixty years later. Spain promised asylum and freedom in Spanish Texas to any slave who escaped from Louisiana or other "foreign" areas. A number of slaves did make it across the Sabine, and there was nothing to be done to legally get them back.

As tensions mounted, U.S. officials took a stiffer stance. At the end of 1805, Secretary of War Henry Dearborn ordered American troops at Natchitoches to go to the nearby Spanish post at Los Adaes, chase any Spaniards found there to the western side of the Sabine River, and to make certain that they stayed west of that river.

Dearborn sent Gen. James Wilkinson to Natchitoches in 1806 to take command of the American troops. When he got to the old Louisiana city, Wilkinson sent a letter to Antonio Cordero, governor of Spanish Texas, telling him that the United States had adopted the Sabine River as the boundary between Louisiana and Texas and demanding that all Spanish troops be pulled back to the river's west side.

Gen. James Wilkinson came to Natchitoches in 1806.

"My sense of high respect which is due from one old soldier to another," Wilkinson wrote, "prohibits the idea of menace; but, as our honor forbids stratagem or deception before our swords have been drawn, I owe it to my own fame, to the national character, to warn you that the ultimate decision of the competent authority has been taken; that my orders are absolute; and my determination fixed, to assert and, under God, to sustain the jurisdiction of the United States to the Sabine River against any force which may be opposed to me.

"Retire then, sir … and spare the effusion of human blood, without prejudicing your own honor, or the substantial interest of His Majesty your Royal master."

Cordero stalled, bluffed, and huffed, but could not do very much else. He believed that Wilkinson could mass troops that would outnumber him two or three to one, would be supported by artillery, and would be much more rested than the Spanish troops that he had been rushing from one place to another. So he leapt at the opportunity when, late in October 1806, Wilkinson made an unexpected proposal: that, until diplomats settled the boundary dispute, the Spanish would remain west of the Sabine River and the Americans east of Arroyo Hondo, several miles to the east of the Sabine, leaving a neutral ground between them that neither force would enter.

The neutral territory became known as No Man's Land, controlled by neither side and policed by neither side. It became such a den of thieves that as late as 1818, travelers such as John Landreth, a surveyor sent from Washington to look for timber in Louisiana, recorded, "[T]hese places, particularly the Mermentau and Calcasu [sic] are the harbours and dens of the most abandoned wretches of the human race … smugglers and pirates who go about the coast of the Gulph [sic] in vessels of small draught of water and rob and plunder without distinction every vessel of every nation they meet and are able to conquer and put to death every soul they find on board without respect of persons age or sex and then their unlawful plunder they carry all through the country and sell at very low rate and find plenty of purchasers."

Finally, in 1819, the United States and Spain signed the Adams-Onis Treaty, which formally set the Sabine River as the boundary between Louisiana and Texas. By that time, however, the question had probably become moot. Eight years before, on February 20, 1811,

President James Madison had signed the bill creating the state of Louisiana and arbitrarily setting the Sabine as its western boundary, No Man's Land notwithstanding.

At the time of the Louisiana Purchase, the Spanish were not the only ones upset at the idea of Louisiana becoming an American possession. So also were many of the natives of New Orleans. They didn't care what happened to the rest of the huge hunk of real estate; they were upset about what was happening on the New Orleans levee and along Canal Street.

For the most part, the Americans who had visited New Orleans in years past were Tennessee and Kentucky flatboatmen who floated down the Mississippi to sell their goods and produce in New Orleans. They were a hard-drinking, loud-cussing, fistfighting lot. And, to the genteel New Orleans Creole ear they were arrogant, loud, rude, and crude. Most of the old New Orleans families were Catholic, at least in name. The so-called "Kaintucks" were Protestant, if they had any religion other than their long rifles and sharp knives.

New Orleans became a city divided at Canal Street. *Les Américains* lived and did business on one side of the street, the French on the other. It is from this arrangement that the term "Dixie" came into being. Boatmen from Kentucky and Tennessee, rich after selling their cargoes flocked to Canal Street. But they had to use French money on the downriver side of the street, American money on the upriver side.

To fix the problem, Citizens' Bank of New Orleans began to issue bilingual bank money. The English word "ten" appeared on one side of the bill, the French "dix" on the other. The boatmen began to call the bills "dixies," and from that, the word became an adjective to describe things of Southern origin and, eventually, the South itself.

Besides the French-American rivalries, the first territorial governor, William Charles Cole Claiborne, had to contend with political and governmental difficulties as well. Louisianians lived under Napoleonic Law, and viewed such things as jury service and voting as impositions as often as they were viewed as privileges. Americans were used to the British Common Law used in all of the other parts of the nation. Court procedures were different, and unfamiliarity bred contempt among the Creoles. Indeed, it could be said that French Creole New Orleans was contemptuous of authority itself, and especially that of a young American.

Claiborne was only twenty-eight years old when he was named governor of the Orleans Territory, and, as Bennett H. Wall points out in his history of Louisiana, the young man had his work cut out for him.

"Claiborne faced a task never before encountered by an American. All previous United States territories had been inhabited in the main by English-speaking Protestants who shared a British tradition of self-government. Claiborne was for the time being virtual dictator over people from radically different cultures who spoke different languages, practiced a different religion from the vast majority of the United States citizens, and had no experience whatsoever with representative government. It was his duty to rule these people justly, to prevent any insurrection against the United States, to introduce them to representative government, and to make them loyal new citizens of a republic which itself was only twenty-seven years old."

Political compromises were made. Ultimately, Louisiana was not forced to adopt the

*William Charles Cole Claiborne, American Louisiana's first territorial governor.*
Courtesy Ouachita Parish
Public Library

English Common Law, and today remains the only state in the Union whose state law is based upon the old Code Napoléon. Claiborne also proved diplomat enough to resolve many of the obvious problems of transition. But the Creoles and the Americans remained like oil and water. They just wouldn't mix — an attitude that spilled over into rural south Louisiana where, well into modern times, *les Américains* were regarded as mercenary, probably dishonest, and certainly nobody for your daughter to marry.

The Territory of Orleans, the part of the Louisiana Purchase that became modern Louisiana, had been reasonably well explored by the time of the sale, but the remaining 800,000 square miles were virtually unknown to Americans. Even before the Purchase, President Jefferson had wanted to explore the vast land. In November 1802, Jefferson asked Don Yrujo if Spain would "take it badly" if the United States sent a small expedition to "explore the course of the Missouri River," which was entirely in Spanish territory before the machinations that led to the Louisiana Purchase.

Yrujo said that Spain would indeed take it quite badly if Americans started roaming around on Spanish lands, but he also knew that Jefferson would probably not take "no" for an answer.

He reported to his superiors in Spain that, "The President has been all his life a man of letters, very speculative and a lover of glory, and it would be possible he might attempt to perpetuate the fame of his administration … by discovering or at least attempting to discover the way by which Americans may some day extend their population and their influence upon the coasts of the South Sea [Pacific Ocean]."

Yrujo had it right. On January 18, 1803, still before he knew about the Louisiana Purchase, Jefferson asked Congress for money for such an excursion, arguing "While other civilized nations have encountered great expense to enlarge the boundaries of knowledge, by undertaking voyages of discovery … our nation [should do the same and] … explore this, the only line of easy communication cross the continent."

When Congress agreed, the president began to discuss the exploration in detail with his thirty-two-year-old Virginia neighbor, Meriwether Lewis, and Lewis's partner, twenty-eight-year-old William Clark. The explorers were in St. Louis making preparations for their journey when the Purchase officially went through, and most of the land they were to explore became U.S. territory.

The famous expedition left St. Louis in the spring of 1804 with forty-eight handpicked men led by a Shoshoni woman with her child strapped to her back. The expedition eventually crossed the Rocky Mountains, descended the Snake and Columbia Rivers, reached the Pacific Coast in the late fall of 1805, and returned to St. Louis in the fall of 1806.

A less-famous expedition did not fare so well. President Jefferson also wanted to explore the Red River, hoping that it would provide a water route to Santa Fe and into the American West. To do that, however, the Americans had to cross territory still disputed by Spain.

Secretary of War Dearborn and Natchez scientist William Dunbar were the organizers of this "Grand Excursion," as Jefferson named it. They began planning in 1804 and Dunbar made a trial run up the Ouachita River during the winter of 1804–1805. He then recruited Thomas Freeman, an astronomer and surveyor, and naturalist Peter Custis to lead the actual expedition.

The Freeman-Custis excursion left Natchez in April 1806, entered the Red River on May 2, and reached Natchitoches a month later. But this expedition soon ran into political difficulty. General Wilkinson, for reasons not entirely clear, told the Spanish government about the American designs on the Red River area. They sent two military expeditions to intercept the American explorers. Freeman and Custis were 615 miles up the river on July 28, when they met a Spanish force under the command of Francisco Viana, who ordered them to turn back. The expedition's turning point in what is now Bowie County, Texas, is still known as Spanish Bluff.

There are many historians who believe that Wilkinson's purpose in telling the Spanish about the expedition was to stir up a shooting war so that he and his friend Aaron Burr, the former vice president of the United States, could take advantage of it.

In 1806, Burr was convinced that war with Spain was inevitable, and thought that he could turn it to his advantage. In July of that year, he paid $5,000 and promised to pay another $35,000 for 400,000 acres of land on the Ouachita River, saying that he planned to put a settlement there. He actually had a much bigger scheme, and, most historians think that Wilkinson had some role in it.

Burr planned to use private troops to take over Texas during the turmoil caused by border fighting between Spain and the United States and to create his own empire there. His plan was foiled because the Spanish did not fight, and there was no turmoil to take advantage of.

Burr was taken to court in May 1807 in one of the most famous trials in America, on charges that his plans constituted treason against the United States. He was eventually acquitted, but not before Jefferson himself attempted to help the court find Burr — a political enemy of the president of long standing — guilty of the charges.

Settlers as well as explorers began to head into the newly acquired U.S. territory immediately after the Louisiana Purchase, hoping to stake out new land and make a beginning for themselves. One of them was a Tennessean named Larkin Edwards, who settled in 1803 near a Caddo Indian village on the Red River. He acted as interpreter for the Caddo as they dealt with fur traders and others who were filtering in growing numbers into the area.

*Former vice president of the United States, Aaron Burr.*

In 1805, Alexander Fulton laid out the plan for the town of Alexandria. There are various stories about how the town was named. One tradition is that it was named for Fulton, another that it was named for his daughter, and yet another holds that it was named for surveyor John Alexander.

In south Louisiana, Acadians were beginning to fan westward from their first homes along Bayou Teche and, as in the northern part of the state, Americans began to filter in, seeking good land in the newly acquired territory.

The census of 1810 showed that the Territory of Orleans, the boot-shaped area that had been separated from the rest of the Louisiana Purchase in 1804, held 76,000 people, almost equally divided among white and black — most of the black people chaffing under the burden of slavery. They had not always borne that burden easily. There were a handful of minor slave rebellions during the French regime, and in 1795 a slave conspiracy in Pointe Coupée Parish was uncovered before the rebellion itself got started.

By the early 1800s, the situation became more critical. There were more slaves than ever in Louisiana, and they were inspired by the success of the slave rebellion in Haiti that overthrew white rule. Despite efforts by Claiborne to maintain order, the largest slave revolt ever to take place in the United States broke out on a plantation about thirty-five miles from New Orleans in 1811.

Not a great deal is known about how the uprising was planned, or even about who all of its leaders were. On January 8, 1811, a slave named Charles led an attack on the Deslondes plantation near the present community of Norco on the east bank of the Mississippi in St. Charles Parish. He and his followers, armed mainly with agricultural implements such as hoes and cane knives, then marched along the river toward New Orleans, freeing slaves from other plantations as they went. Their plan was to march into the city and free the slaves there.

By January 10, the mob, numbering as many as 500 slaves, was just ten miles from the city when they ran into strong opposition from a group of federal troops, militiamen, and vigilantes. Sixty-six of the slaves were killed in the melee. Sixteen of the leaders were captured, tried by court-martial in New Orleans, and executed. So ended the last slave revolt in Louisiana history.

Since the 1810 census showed that the population of the Territory of Orleans was well above the 60,000 needed to apply for statehood, Julian Poydras, the Orleans territory's delegate to Congress proposed that the eighteenth state be created. Legislation was passed on February 20, 1811, setting up a convention in New Orleans in November 1811 to draw up a state constitution. Forty-five delegates met that month to draft the document, and Louisiana became a state on April 30, 1812.

The newest American state found trouble right away.

Thirty-two days after Louisiana was granted statehood, the United States declared war on England, primarily because of British naval practices — including snatching American seamen and forcing them to serve on British ships — during renewed fighting between France and Great Britain. That declaration put Louisiana, the guardian of the mouth of the Mississippi River, in a precarious position, particularly after 1814, when Britain defeated Napoléon in France and could concentrate on America.

British planners decided to attack the United States at three key points: Niagara and Lake Champlain in the north, and New Orleans in the south. New Orleans was not even close to being ready to defend itself against a determined attack by one of the best fighting forces in the world.

Fifty British ships gathered in Jamaica during the fall of 1814 in preparation for an attack on New Orleans. On board were 10,000 men, as well as civil officials who planned to take over the government of Louisiana after what they expected to be an easy battle. Meanwhile, Gen. Andrew Jackson and a handful of militiamen moved into New Orleans

Following page:
*Oil painting "The Battle of New Orleans" by Louis Eugene L'Ami, 1839.*
Courtesy Louisiana State Museum.

to organize the best defenses they could. The British didn't know it, but that organization included an alliance with a man of some notoriety in New Orleans — the pirate Jean Lafitte.

Lafitte commanded an enclave of smugglers—many of whom had been veterans of Napoléon's wars on the continent — at Barataria Bay, an arm of the Gulf of Mexico below New Orleans. They had cannons, they had ammunition, and they had trained manpower — all of which Jackson desperately needed.

When the British arrived off the Louisiana coast, they offered Lafitte an officer's rank if he would throw in with them. Instead, he went to New Orleans, met with the Louisiana officials there, told them about the British offer, and said that he would instead fight with the Americans — if they would have him.

The Americans were not interested at first. Lafitte and his smugglers had been a thorn in the side of Governor Claiborne since his first days in office, thumbing their respective noses at American customs officials as they brought contraband of every sort to the city. Jackson regarded Lafitte as no better than a thief and pirate.

But, in the end, they looked at his batteries of cannon, his casks of gunpowder, his rifles and riflemen, and decided they'd better accept his offer, if for no other reason than to keep him from adding his strength to that of the British.

The two forces began to skirmish just before Christmas 1814, but the big British attack came on January 8, 1815, near Chalmette, south of New Orleans. Line after regimented line

of red-coated British soldiers marched against the ragtag army hidden behind hastily built earthworks. Jackson's militiamen, woodsmen all, were crack rifle shots. Lafitte's cannoneers, trained by Napoléon and kept in practice through piracy, knew how to handle their weapons.

The British finally broke and ran. Their losses were in the thousands. American losses were in the hundreds.

The British stayed in the area, threatening to attack again, until January 18, when they climbed back aboard their ships and sailed away. Ironically, the great Battle of New Orleans should not have been fought. The United States and Great Britain signed the Treaty of Ghent, ending the war, two weeks before, but word had not filtered by then into the bayou country.

## CHAPTER THREE

# Steamboat Days

*he New Orleans, the first steamboat* to descend the Mississippi to its namesake city, arrived on January 12, 1812. That event changed not only the commerce of the entire Mississippi River, but also the history of all of Louisiana.

Until the coming of the steamboat, water travel on the Mississippi and on the other navigable waterways within Louisiana was all driven by muscle or wind. Flatboats traveling down the Mississippi were torn up and sold for their lumber in New Orleans because it was too hard to get them back upriver against the current.

Waterways had long been Louisiana's highways. Navigable streams ran to every section of the state and the French and Spanish — as had the Native Americans before them — used this network of waterways as their principal means of travel and commerce.

The Mississippi River was, of course, Louisiana's major highway, and a major highway for all of middle America. But Louisiana was also blessed with other rivers that opened the way to travel and trade. People at first traveled these waterways by bateaux, rafts, pirogues, and other small boats.

Almost immediately, and particularly from 1830 to 1880, fleets of steamboats began to operate on every river in the state — some of them magnificent palaces carrying plantation owners and the idle rich up and down the Mississippi, most of them much simpler affairs designed to carry cotton, sugar, hogs, and cattle alongside their human cargo.

Warehouses and storage sheds, then hotels and inns began to develop around steamboat stops, and many of them continued to develop into towns and cities that we know today.

At the beginning of the steamboat era, the Red River was open all year as far as Alexandria, but low water often kept all but the smallest boats from going farther upriver. The Black, Ouachita, and smaller streams of the Red River system were open to steamboat traffic only when the water was high enough.

In the Florida parishes, the Amite, Tangipahoa, the Tchefuncte and the Pearl Rivers were navigable most of the time to small craft, and the lakes around New Orleans — Pontchartrain,

Opposite page: *The steamer America on the Mississippi River.*
Courtesy Noel Memorial Library Archives, LSU in Shreveport

*Cotton traffic on the levee, New Orleans, circa 1907.*
Courtesy Noel Memorial Library Archives, LSU in Shreveport PC350:

Milburne's Studio photo

Maurepas, and Borgne, were busy with steam craft.

Bayou Lafourche and Bayou Teche were the major routes in south Louisiana. Bayou Plaquemine branched off of the Mississippi River and connected to the Atchafalaya, providing a convoluted route to such inland ports as Washington in St. Landry Parish, and also offered an even more circuitous route to connect to Bayou Teche.

Farther west were the Vermilion, Mermentau, Calcasieu, and Sabine Rivers, all of them navigable to points well inland.

In 1819, the steamboat James Monroe was the first to ascend the Ouachita River to the little settlement at Fort Miró. The local residents apparently recognized that it was an auspicious occasion. After a delegation headed by Judge Henry Bry visited the little steamer, they decided to honor the boat by changing the name of their settlement. Fort Miró became Monroe.

Most historians date the era of steamboat traffic in south Louisiana also to 1819, when François Duplessis Jr.'s steamboat *Louisiana* chugged up Bayou Teche to New Iberia.

In 1832, Captain Henry Miller Shreve, a hero of the War of 1812, cleared the Red River of the "Great Raft" — a huge log jam that stretched for more than 160 miles and made the river unnavigable. He had been hired by the federal government to clear the river because moving military supplies overland was too difficult.

By 1835, Shreve had reached the Caddo Indian settlement about nine miles south of the heart of present-day Shreveport at the Peach Bottom bluff on Bayou Pierre. That same year, the Caddo Indians sold all but 640 acres of their land to the federal government for $80,000 and moved west. They gave the 640 acres that they reserved to their old interpreter and friend, Larkin Edwards, who later sold it to the Shreve Town Company for $5,000.

*Steamer "Natchez" at the levee, New Orleans, circa 1900.*
Courtesy Noel Memorial Library Archives, LSU in Shreveport PB182

The eight men who made up the company included William Bennet, James Cane, Angus McNeill, Bushrod Jenkins, Thomas Sprague, Thomas Williamson, James Pickett, and Captain Shreve. Each of them agreed to pay part of the cost of building a "suitable house for public entertainment, steam saw mill, and such other improvements as may be deemed necessary to advance the prosperity of the town."

Commerce Street, along the river, was the first and busiest to be developed in Shreveport. And, showing already its close alliance with the Lone Star State, three of the early streets were named for heroes of the Alamo (Fannin, Travis, and Crockett) and a fourth was named for Texas itself.

*Sugar levee, New Orleans, circa 1900.*
Courtesy Noel Memorial Library Archives, LSU in Shreveport PC341

*The steamer U. S. Aid and a crew of workers labor to clear a raft in the Red River, 1873.*
Courtesy Noel Memorial Library Archives, LSU in Shreveport PA1651 & PA1680: R. B. Talfor, photographer

In 1837, the first railroad west of the Mississippi River, the Red River Line, was built to connect Cheneyville and Alexandria, hauling mostly sugar and cotton to steamboats on the river, but railroads would come later to much of Louisiana than to other states, particularly in south Louisiana. Railroad men thought south Louisiana's marshy terrain made track laying either impossible or prohibitively expensive. As late 1914, for example, when railroads were being built across the nation, the U.S. Secretary of War suggested in a report to Congress that canals be constructed in south Louisiana instead of trying to lay track.

He wrote, "The land is of such character and so cut by bayous and lakes, that railroad construction is impossible, and no other method of communication than by water is practicable."

Even the idea of building canals in south Louisiana seemed a little bit silly at first glance. Some places appeared to be more water than land. But most of the rivers and bayous ran in a north-south direction, and, even with the maze of waterways, it was difficult to move from east to west.

*Steamer boats owned by the Texas and Pacific Railroad, Shreveport, 1900.*
Courtesy Noel Memorial Library Archives, LSU in Shreveport

*The stern-wheeled steamboat Borealis Rex provided a vital link of transportation and communication between Lake Charles and Leesburg (Cameron).*
Courtesy Murphy Library, University of Wisconsin-LaCrosse

*Steamer City of Monroe.*
Courtesy Noel Memorial Library Archives, LSU in Shreveport PC247: Earl M. Norman Studio, Natches, Miss

Thomas A. Becnel noted in a history of south Louisiana water commerce, "The real transportation barrier was east-west linkups to settlements separated by salt or freshwater marsh. To get from one community to another on a nearby bayou just a few miles across the marsh, a settler sometimes had to travel a great distance. He could descend one stream to the Gulf and then ascend an adjacent stream. Or he could ascend the stream on which his settlement lay until he reached a main branch upstream. … When possible, settlers cut pirogue trails or ditches, which the French called *trainasses* through the marsh. … The ditches [became] narrow, shallow canals. In time these grew into canals that were used for drainage, transportation, logging, trapping, and petroleum production in the twentieth century."

Steamboats probably did not begin regular routes on the Vermilion River, which is navigable from the Gulf of Mexico to Lafayette, as early as on some other south Louisiana streams. That was partly because it was relatively easy to move goods by wagon from Bayou Teche steamboat stops at New Iberia and St. Martinville, and partly because trade

*Steamboat landing, New Orleans, circa 1910.*
Courtesy Noel Memorial Library Archives, LSU in Shreveport PB216

along the Teche, which was lined with sugar plantations, was much more lucrative than along the sparsely settled Vermilion.

Steamers were venturing up the Vermilion at least as far as Abbeville by the time of the Civil War, and it is probable that by then they were coming all the way to Vermilionville, as Lafayette was then called.

To the west, the prairies along the Mermentau River were all but empty of settlement until the coming of the railroads in the 1880s, which grabbed most of the commerce. But a few little steamboats did haul rice, cotton, cattle, and lumber from the area into the early 1900s.

The *Amy Hewes,* owned and operated by the Hewes Lumber Company of Jeanerette, was probably the last steamboat to operate in southern Louisiana, and perhaps all of the state. She was taken out of service in 1943. A few paddle-wheel boats continued to operate even later than that, but these were powered by diesel engines, not by steam.

*Unloading bales of cotton from the steamer America in the early 1900s.*
Courtesy Louisiana State Archives

## CHAPTER FOUR

1861 - 1866

# Look Away, Louisiana

*M*ore than 56,000 men from Louisiana carried
Confederate arms during the Civil War and another 10,000 boys and older men were
part of the so-called home guard. More than 600 battles, skirmishes, and raids took
place within the state during the war, although only a handful of them gained more than
passing attention in the history books.

Louisiana troops fought all across the
South in some of the bloodiest battles of the
war. The state furnished four Confederate
generals of note — P. G. T. Beauregard, Braxton
Bragg, Leonidas Polk, and Richard Taylor.

In Louisiana, the first official steps
toward war came on January 26, 1861, when a
secession convention voted 113 to 17 to declare
Louisiana a "free and independent power."

*Oil painting
"Louisiana Seccession
Convention," 1861,
by Enoch Wood
Perry.*
Courtesy Louisiana State Museum

Former Louisiana Gov. Alexandre Mouton of Vermilionville (Lafayette) presided over that
convention. Typical of the "two Louisianas" that existed even then, Louisiana was the only
state whose secession ordinance was adopted in both French and English.

Three months later, on March 21, Louisiana gave up its "freedom and independence"
and joined with other secessionist states to form the Confederate States of America.

The act of secession was hardly more than a formality. It was the talk of the state
even before the election in November 1860 of President Abraham Lincoln, who had such
little backing in Louisiana that his name wasn't even on the state ballot. Southern Democrat
John C. Breckinridge of Kentucky led Louisiana in 1860 with 22,861 votes. He beat the
Constitutional Union party's John Bell of Tennessee, who got 20, 204 votes. Northern
Democrat Stephen O. Douglas of Illinois got just over 7,600 votes in the state.

There was immediate reaction across the South to Lincoln's election. Political leaders
such as Louisiana Gov. Thomas Overton Moore saw it as the last straw in a sure fight
between the abolitionist North and the slaveholding South.

*Opposite: The bom-
bardment of Port
Hudson – 100-pound
Parrott gun of the
Richmond at work.*
Courtesy Ouachita Parish
Public Library

"Our enemies who have driven ... their conflict with the slaveholding states to the extremity will have found that throughout the borders of Louisiana we are one people," he told the legislature on January 22, 1861, "a people with one heart and one mind, who will not be cajoled into an abandonment of their rights, and who cannot be subdued."

> **❝ ...we are one people, a people with one heart and one mind, who will not be cajoled into an abandonment of their rights and who cannot be subdued.❞**
>
> — Gov. Thomas Overton Moore

His rhetoric may have mirrored the minds of the legislators, but it may not have been so reflective of the views of the common man. To begin with, the people of Louisiana never voted for secession, they voted only for delegates to a secession convention. And some historians, such as Jefferson Davis Bragg, point out that many of the people did not even vote for the delegates, thinking the vote was loaded anyway.

"The fact should not be overlooked," Bragg writes in his *Louisiana in the Confederacy,* "that the vote for delegates to the [secession] convention was 12,766 less than the total number of votes cast in the Louisiana presidential election in November. ... It seems reasonable to conclude ... that the failure of a considerable percentage of the qualified voters to exercise the privilege in this case was not due ... to a lack of interest. The issues were too well defined; and the campaign ... was too heated to result in indifference or apathy. Somehow, the writer cannot escape the opinion that these twelve thousand nonvoting citizens represented in a large degree an opposition to the whole movement of secession, that they were Union men who stayed away from the polls as a means of protest against the seemingly inevitable withdrawal of Louisiana from the Union, either separately or in a united Southern movement."

But, whatever the popular sentiment before secession, once the confrontation came, Louisiana men were among the first to join. The state had been raising troops since March 9, 1861, when Confederate Secretary of War Leroy Pope Walker asked for 1,700 men to help protect once-Federal forts that had been seized by the Confederacy. President Jefferson Davis asked for another 3,000 troops on April 8.

That would be just the beginning. There was a call for another 5,000 troops from Louisiana on April 15, for 5,000 more on April 21. By the middle of 1861, Louisiana had more than 8,000 men in active service and another 16,000 in training. And as quickly as they mustered the basics, they were shipped off to fight in the first engagements of the war. By the end of 1861, some 18,000 Louisianians were under arms and scattered throughout the South — and that turned out to be a problem, a big problem. With all of these men gone elsewhere, and more to follow them, there were not enough men and guns left to protect Louisiana — despite the fact that Louisiana was one of the most strategically important spots in the South.

The single fact that the mouth of the Mississippi River lies in Louisiana ensured the state's importance to both the Union and the Confederacy. Each side wanted to control the river, since it was America's busiest waterway in a time and place when waterways were still the most important avenues of travel.

Almost the first strategy proposed by Lt. Gen. Winfield Scott, general-in-chief of the Union Army, was to take control of the Mississippi River and split the Confederacy. Then he would attempt to strangle the South into submission with a naval blockade that would keep Southern ships locked in port and prevent needed supplies from reaching the South.

Two decrepit forts, Fort Jackson on the west bank of the river and Fort St. Philip on the east, were all that stood between the Union and control of the lower Mississippi. Cannon and men were rushed to the old forts, and a boom made of huge cypress logs chained together was stretched across the river between the two forts to stop any Union ships that tried to run between them. Eight old schooners were anchored behind the logs to create a bigger barrier. Forty or fifty rafts loaded with pine logs and soaked with turpentine were put in front of the blockade, to be set afire if necessary.

Before Federal ships could run by Fort Jackson and Fort St. Phillip, they would have to run through the line of burning rafts, break the chain barrier, and run past the line of old schooners, which could also be set afire.

A Union fleet commanded by Flag Officer David Farragut entered the river in early 1862 and proposed to run that gauntlet. He brought his own firepower: 17 big men-of-war, 20 mortar boats, and 7 smaller gunboats — 268 guns of various sizes and styles altogether.

The mortar boats began a barrage of the forts on Good Friday, April 18, at 10 a.m. Over the next six days, 7,500 bombs and shells were fired into the forts. Then, at 2 a.m. on April 24, Farragut gave the order for the Federal ships to try to run up the river and through the barriers between the forts.

One of the Confederates defending the fort wrote after the battle, "It was so dark we could see nothing; but as the the second rocket faded, in one instant the whole scene was brilliantly illuminated as if by magic. Every gun opened in the forts, the vessels poured broadside after broadside [lighting the scene so that] we could see every yard, every sail, every rope, every man

*Oil painting of Farragut's Fleet Passing the Forts Below New Orleans. Mauritz F. H. de Haas, circa 1866.*
Courtesy Historic
New Orleans Collection

in the rigging, every man at the guns in the Forts, dark against the red sulphurous light. The men working the little howitzers in the rigging of the Hartford looked like black imps or devils clinging and climbing about her ropes. It was the most superb sight I ever witnessed — so flashing, so bewildering, so magnificent, so brief."

The Federal boats crashed through the barrier, past the burning barges, under the guns of the fort. The fighting was all over by dawn. Fort Jackson and Fort St. Philip were still there, but now they were useless. Farragut had run his fleet past them and there was nothing

*Union Maj. Gen.*
*Benjamin Butler*

to stop him from sailing up the river to a New Orleans thrown into panic by the news of the outcome of the fight.

Farragut's gunboats reached New Orleans by 2 p.m. The river was running high — almost at the top of the levee guarding the low-lying city — so that the Federal guns could be trained, unobstructed on the heart of the city. Confederate Maj. Gen. Mansfield Lovell had fewer than 5,000 troops to guard New Orleans. He loaded them on a train and saved them to fight another day. U.S. Maj. Gen. Benjamin Butler moved into New Orleans and began a stringent military rule that earned him the wrath of the people and the nickname "Beast Butler."

One of his first objectives after taking firm control of New Orleans was to secure the lower Mississippi River for the Stars and Stripes. This was part of the larger Union strategy of controlling the river as a means of strangling the Confederacy. But Union control of the lower Mississippi had a side effect. It isolated south Louisiana's barely defended bayou country.

Lt. Gen. Edmund Kirby Smith, who had command of Confederate forces west of the Mississippi River, placed that defense in the hands of Maj. Gen. Richard Taylor, a Louisiana native and son of former President Zachary Taylor. General Taylor was described by one of his soldiers as "a quiet, unassuming little fellow, but noisy on retreats, with a tendency to cuss mules and wagons which stall on the road."

If that was the case, Taylor had a lot of opportunity for cussing. In October 1862, he counted fewer than 5,000 men under his command, and about half of them did not have a working weapon. And he would spend a lot of time going backward, fighting rear-guard action after rear-guard action while Federal troops pushed through south Louisiana.

In November 1862, Maj. Gen. Nathaniel Banks relieved Butler in Federal command in New Orleans, bringing the second major player onto the scene in what would become the battle for the bayou country. Before the war ended, he and Taylor faced each other at the Mississippi, at the Teche, at the Atchafalaya, at the Red, and along and near practically every other Louisiana waterway big enough for Banks to bring a gunboat. Banks had 40,000 well-equipped men to pitch against Taylor's ill-equipped 5,000.

Banks came to New Orleans with orders to take Port Hudson, twenty miles upriver from Baton Rouge, and then to join Maj. Gen. Ulysses S. Grant in a campaign against Vicksburg. These were the last two Confederate strongholds on the Mississippi, and if they fell into Union hands, the entire length of the river would be under Federal control.

But Banks had a problem, in the form of 1,500 or so Confederates under the command of Brig. Gen. Alfred Mouton, who were lurking across the river from New Orleans, using hit-and-run tactics to keep the Union forces off balance. Banks feared that if he pulled enough men out of New Orleans to march up the Mississippi and take control of Port Hudson, that Mouton would slip across the river and regain control of the Crescent City.

Banks decided he had to deal with Mouton before he dealt with Port Hudson. In late

*Confederate Maj. Gen.*
*Richard Taylor*

*Union Maj. Gen.*
*Nathaniel Banks*

October 1862, he sent Brig. Gen. Godfrey Weitzel across the Mississippi and down Bayou Lafourche with 4,000 Union soldiers. At the same time, Union gunboats sailed from New Orleans, headed for Brashear City, as Morgan City was called then. The plan was for Weitzel to drive Mouton's army back to the Atchafalaya River, where he would be trapped by the gunboats.

And it almost worked. Mouton fought stubbornly as he backed along the only railroad track in south Louisiana — running from Algiers (on the west bank of the Mississippi across from New Orleans) to Brashear City. He made it across the Atchafalaya just before the Federal gunboats arrived. Had they not been delayed by low tides and bad weather, the trap would have worked exactly as planned.

But even though he was across the Atchafalaya, Mouton was forced to continue to back away, up the Teche. He made a stand at a ring of dirt that hardly qualified for its name of Fort Bisland, near present-day Patterson, and narrowly escaped a Federal trap there. Then, during the spring of 1863, the Confederates fought a delaying action up Bayou Teche, through Franklin and Jeanerette, New Iberia, Vermilionville, and Opelousas and, by late spring, on to Alexandria. Only then did Banks feel secure enough to turn his attention to Port Hudson.

Banks thought it would be a relatively easy job of taking the place. Again, he far outnumbered the 7,000 Confederate forces hunkered down in the fort, and had a wide-open supply line from New Orleans. But, unfortunately for him, Port Hudson was a place made for defense. It sat atop a sixty-foot bluff on the Mississippi's east side, at a place where the river made a sharp bend so that boats running below the fort were exposed to blistering Confederate cannon fire. Adding to the natural defenses, the countryside nearby was cut by ravines deep enough to stop men and horses, and Confederate engineers had built earthworks to enhance the natural terrain.

Maj. Gen. Franklin Gardner, the brother-in-law of General Mouton,

*Confederate Brig. Gen. Alfred Mouton*
Courtesy Lafayette Museum

*Battle of Baton Rouge as sketched from the camp of the Indiana Regiment.*
Courtesy Ouachita Parish Public Library

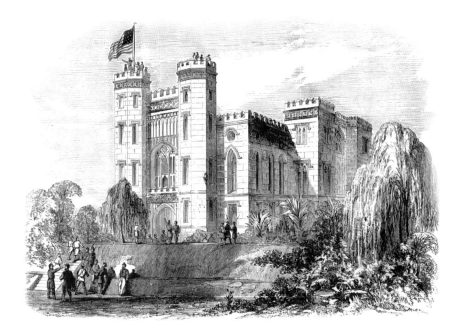

commanded the fort at Port Hudson. And if Mouton had been pesky in designing hit-and-run tactics, Gardner was just plain stubborn.

Banks began his attack with an artillery barrage just after dawn on May 27, 1863. Then he sent wave after wave of troops against the Confederate lines. The fighting was intense, and bloody. It ended at 6 p.m., twelve hours after it had begun. There were 300 Confederate casualties. Banks counted 2,000. For all

*Banks's expedition – executive officer Parker, of the Union gunboat Essex, hoists the United States flag on the state capitol, Baton Rouge, December 17, 1863.*
Courtesy Louisiana State Archives

of the blood, the Union gained only a few yards of ground and wrecked a few Confederate cannons.

During the weeks after the bloody battle of May 27, Port Hudson continued to see some of the grimmest fighting of the Civil War before Banks finally realized that head-on attacks would get him nothing. When he began an almost continuous artillery barrage, the Confederates dug deeper into the ground and held on. Stubborn Franklin Gardner would not surrender.

On Saturday, June 13, Banks and his artillery commander, Brig. Gen. Richard Arnold, decided upon a simple new plan: They would just blast Port Hudson to pieces.

Arnold massed 116 cannon in front of the fort and began to fire away. At the peak of the bombardment, shells were falling inside Port Hudson at the rate of one per second. When the cannons quit firing, Federal riflemen moved toward the apparently lifeless fort. They were within sixty yards of the outer lines when, as they had done before, hundreds of grim Confederate riflemen reared up from the holes where they had been hiding, opened a withering fire, and sent the surprised Union soldiers scurrying back to their own lines.

Banks lined up gunboats on the river and began an all-night barrage from that side. Later he blasted away from both the land and the water. Surely, he thought, that would do the trick. He sent 3,000 men rushing against the fort. This time they got within twenty feet of the Confederate defenders. But that was as close as they would come.

Port Hudson held out until Independence Day, July 4, 1863, and would have held out longer. But on that day the word arrived that Grant had taken Vicksburg and was bringing thousands more soldiers to help Banks finish the job at Port Hudson. The Confederates had no food, little ammunition. On July 8, the Confederate troops, reduced to fewer than 3,000 men, laid down their arms. The battered fort had withstood sixty days of bombardment by the Federal river fleet and forty-eight days of actual siege.

Meanwhile, the stubborn defense at Port Hudson allowed other Confederate forces to almost do what Banks had feared: regain New Orleans. General Taylor decided that the best thing he could do to relieve Port Hudson was to "capture the [Brashear City] fortifications, overrun [Bayou] Lafourche, interrupt Banks' communication with New Orleans, and threaten the city itself."

Taylor assembled 3,000 men in Alexandria and sent a 650-man cavalry unit under Col. J. P. Major toward Algiers by way of Opelousas, Plaquemine, and Thibodaux. General Mouton and cavalry officer Brig. Gen. Thomas Green took the rest of the army down Bayou Teche to Brashear City. The plan was to capture both ends of the southern railroad that ran from Algiers to Brashear City, and then to use it to amass the men and materiel needed to cross the Mississippi and fight their way into New Orleans.

By the end of June, Brashear City had been retaken and the Confederate army was in control of a substantial segment of the west bank of the Mississippi just above New Orleans. But, they were just a little bit too late; Vicksburg and Port Hudson fell before they could consolidate their gains, and Banks was able to rush men down the river to mount a defense. By the end of July the overwhelming Federal forces had regained Brashear City and driven Taylor's forces away from the Mississippi.

Banks made his own way back to New Orleans, but not for long.

By the fall of 1863, rumors reached Washington that French Emperor Louis Napoléon (Napoléon III), whose troops held most of Mexico, was planning to take over Texas, and possibly Louisiana, too. President Abraham Lincoln feared that, at the least, he would send men or supplies to aid the Confederate cause. He told Banks to go to Texas and make sure

*Unloading military stores at the levee in Baton Rouge from the Union transport North Star over the Mississippi steamer Iberville.*

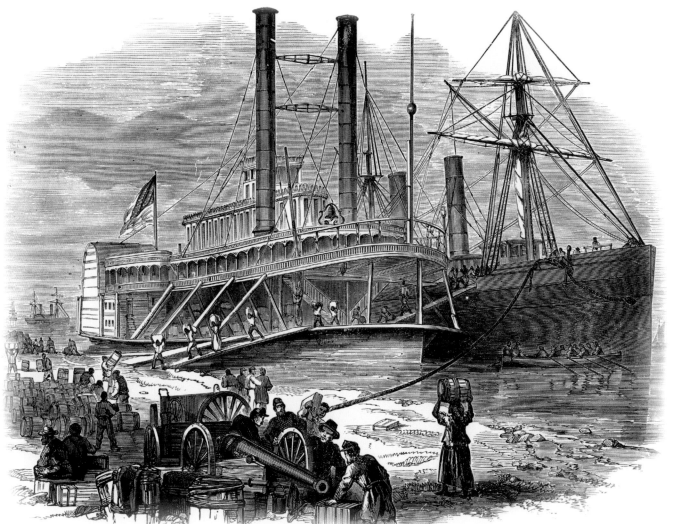

that no Confederate-French linkup happened.

Union Gen. William B. Franklin was given field command of the Great Overland Expedition, as the march to Texas was called. He took with him fifty-one infantry regiments, fourteen cavalry regiments, seventeen artillery batteries, six engineer regiments, and all the supporting personnel for these troops. Taylor sent the pesky General Mouton to block Franklin's way. Mouton had 9,000 men on paper, only half of that actually present and able to fight.

The Union troops rode the rails to Brashear City and began to march up the Teche from there on October 2, passing again through the communities they had pillaged in the spring — this time taking anything that had been overlooked on the first trip through.

Mouton tried his hit-and-run tactics, but the massive Federal army just kept moving until it reached Vermilionville, where the original plan had been to turn west, march across the southwest Louisiana prairies, and cross into Texas at Niblett's Bluff, just west of Vinton.

But by the time his army got to Vermilionville, Banks was having second thoughts. He far outnumbered the Confederate troops defending the area. But there were some fine Texas cowboys in the Confederate cavalry. They were good riders on good horses. Most of Banks's men were on foot. He was afraid — and rightfully so — that the Texans would decimate his foot soldiers with hit-and-run raids on horseback if he tried to cross the prairies of southwest Louisiana.

Banks decided instead to continue north from Vermilionville to Alexandria, and then to follow the Red River to Shreveport. That way, the river would protect his flank and Union gunboats on the river would give him more firepower.

While his men spent the winter in the Teche country, Banks revised his plan, turning it into a joint operation with Maj. Gen. William T. Sherman, commander of Union troops in Mississippi, and Maj. Gen. Frederick Steele, who was in charge of the Federal army in Arkansas.

Banks planned to move up Bayou Teche with 17,000 troops and link up in Alexandria in the middle of March with 10,000 troops that Sherman was to bring up the Red River. Steele

*View of Alexandria before the destruction of the town by fire, during General Banks's raid, 1863.*
Courtesy Noel Memorial Library Archives, LSU in Shreveport PC321

was to bring another 15,000 men south from Little Rock and join Banks as he marched toward Shreveport. At the same time, a Union naval fleet under the command of Admiral David D. Porter was to travel up the Red in conjunction with the army, adding still more firepower.

The Confederate commanders knew what was going on. When it became obvious that Banks was preparing to move up the Red in force, the Confederate command strengthened defenses along the river from Shreveport to Fort DeRussy, which was about three miles north of Marksville. But there wasn't much to strengthen them with.

Shreveport was guarded by a dozen small artillery posts ringing the city and by Fort Turnbull, Fort Jenkins, and Fort Albert Sidney Johnston. They were well situated for defense, if they'd had cannons and ammunition. But both were in woefully short supply. At Fort Turnbull, according to anecdotal accounts, logs were charred in campfires and mounted on the fort walls, disguised to look like cannons. When Confederate Maj. Gen. John B. Magruder inspected the place, he remarked that the fort was "only so much humbug." The name stuck and Fort Turnbull became Fort Humbug.

Two Union divisions landed at Simmesport on March 13 and moved through Marksville and toward Fort DeRussy the next day. Porter brought his gunships up next to the fort and began to blast away, but the Union commanders told him to stop. The fort's Confederate defenders were so outnumbered that Porter was more likely to hit friend than foe.

By March 18, the Union force was reinforced with the arrival of 15,000 troops under General Franklin, who had slogged the muddy trail up the Teche and then into central Louisiana. There were at least 30,000 men ready to march by March 24, when Banks arrived in Alexandria and took personal command of the expedition. Maybe he shouldn't have, because he made a big blunder.

Part of his original plan had been to march along the Red where Porter's gunboats could protect him. But, for some reason, perhaps because he'd met only light opposition on his trek toward Shreveport, he decided to veer away from the river and take a shortcut. Just past Natchitoches, he turned his army down a narrow, tree-lined dirt road.

The woods alongside this road were so dense that the Union artillery had no place to set up. The Federal cavalry leading the march was hemmed in by the trees and had no room to maneuver. Just behind the cavalry were 300 supply wagons pulled by six-mule teams that could not turn around in narrow places. The wagons blocked the road so that the infantry troops behind them could not get to the front quickly. There were more wagons behind the infantry, blocking the way if they had to retreat. And, to top it all, a heavy rain turned the road into something "more like a broad, deep, red-colored ditch than anything else," according to one Federal diarist.

At mid-afternoon April 8, the cavalrymen at the head of the long Federal column rode out of the piney woods and onto the rim of a large clearing with a broad, low hill at the center. Eleven thousand Confederate soldiers were hidden in the woods beyond the clearing.

Here, at Sabine Crossroads, near Mansfield in DeSoto Parish, General Taylor had finally found what he'd been looking for: a situation in which he had the advantage. He had the advantage of position, he had the advantage of surprise, and because Union soldiers were jammed along a narrow, muddy road, he could bring more men into the

fray than Banks could.

Just after four o'clock, when the first elements of the long Federal column began to emerge from the woods and into the clearing, Taylor sent reinforcements to General Mouton's 18th Louisiana Infantry on the Confederate left, and told him to attack.

Mouton's troops attacked like "infuriated devils," according to one Union diarist.

A journalist traveling with the Union column wrote, "Suddenly, there was a rush, a shout, a crashing of trees, the breaking down of rails, the rush and scamper of men. It was sudden as though a thunderbolt had fallen among us, and set the pines on fire. I turned to my companion to inquire the reason of this extraordinary proceeding, but before he had the chance to reply, we found ourselves swallowed up, as it were, in a hissing, seething, bubbling whirlpool of agitated men."

The Battle of Mansfield and a fight the next day at Pleasant Hill turned the tide in Louisiana. The Federal march toward Texas was stopped, and the Union was forced to retreat. The Great Texas Overland Expedition had turned into a federal disaster. But it was not without its cost, including the loss of General Mouton, who was killed in the battle, and without the loss of much of Alexandria which was set afire as the Federal troops fled from the city.

Banks was eventually able to get his men and equipment in order and to make an orderly retreat. But Admiral Porter had a tougher time of it on the river. Practically his entire fleet, one of the biggest ever assembled west of the Mississippi River, was upriver from the rapids at Alexandria, and getting the boats back to the deep water of the Mississippi River would be no easy trick.

First, he had to get to the rapids, a challenge in itself, because the river had been dropping and in many places was low enough to strand some of his bigger boats.

Porter needed seven feet of water to get his big boats past the rapids at Alexandria. When he got back downriver to the city, the channel held just a little more than three feet at its deepest point. Porter was willing to try anything, when Lt. Col. Joseph Bailey came to him with a proposition that, Porter wrote, "looked like madness." Bailey wanted to build a series of dams across the river, letting the water pool behind them until it was deep enough to float the boats across the Rapids.

Porter persuaded Banks to give Bailey 3,000 men and 400 wagons and teams. Bailey began his work on April 30, toppling trees into the river, building huge boxes to be put into the water and filled with logs and stones and anything else that could be found. Two barges were placed in the middle, to act as "doors" so that they could be opened when the water was high enough and Porter's fleet could rush through.

The dam gave way on May 9, but not before a pool of water had built up behind them. When Porter saw what was happening, he rushed to his biggest boats, lined them up, and ran them through the opening. Bailey was then able to repair the dam enough for the rest of the boats to get through.

With the boats saved, Banks's Union army marched out of the smoking ruins of Alexandria on May 13, chased and harassed by Confederates. They skirmished at Mansura, and Taylor nearly trapped them before they could get across the Mississippi, but — as always — it was an "almost" thing.

After the Red River campaign there were no important operations by either side in Louisiana. The Confederate forces in the state held on until the end of the war, then took their mules and muskets home, or to whatever remained of home. Historians estimate that fully half of the wealth of the state — railroads, plantations, farm buildings, livestock, mills, stores and their goods — was stolen, torn down, burned, or ransacked. One-fifth of the men who fought for the Confederacy were killed.

*Porter's gunboats passing the dam in the Red River near Alexandria, June 1864.*

Courtesy Noel Memorial Library Archives, LSU in Shreveport PC330

## CHAPTER FIVE

1867 - 1900

# Reconstruction & Railroads

*O*nly three states, Virginia, South Carolina, and Georgia, suffered more destruction than did Louisiana during the Civil War, and the impact of those losses would continue for many years to come — and indeed there would be further looting to come.

And, even though the war was over, the reasons for the fighting did not simply go away. With economic chaos came other disturbances. Civil authority all but disappeared or was disobeyed when Southerners thought harsh penalties were being imposed upon them. Poverty breeds crime, and outlaws were everywhere. Vagrants, black and white, either dismissed from the army with nothing in their pockets and no place to go, or from the plantation in similar circumstances, roamed the countryside, seeking food and shelter where they could find it, and by any way they could get it.

The political situation was just as chaotic. A constitutional convention abolished slavery in Louisiana, but did not give the freed men full citizenship rights. Most of them still could not vote, so a government and legislature fully in sympathy with the old Confederate cause went back into office and dominated the political scene until the passage of the Federal Reconstruction Act of 1867.

This act divided the South into five districts, denied the vote to former Confederates and Confederate sympathizers, and gave the vote to black males. Under it, 82,907 blacks and 44,732 whites were registered to vote and from that time until 1890 blacks continued to dominate the voter registration.

The disenfranchised white people resisted the Reconstruction rules, sometimes through legal, political means, more often through other ways, using such organizations as the Knights of the White Camellia, Ku Klux Klan, and other secret societies to achieve by terror what they could not through the political process.

As Edwin Adams Davis put it, "It was a period of almost constant disorder. … Radical white and colored political leaders systematically looted the state. Carpetbaggers flocked to Louisiana from northern states with frenzied desire for power and spoils, and scalawag Louisianians joined with them. … Loyal Louisianians were frequently forced to operate outside the law to preserve a semblance of order. … Radical leaders organized the

*Pickney Benton Stewart Pinchback served as governor from December 9, 1872 to January 13, 1873, when Governor Warmoth was impeached. Pinchback was the first Black to hold the position of governor.*
Courtesy Louis J. Perret, Clerk of Court, Lafayette Parish

**Opposite page:** *Kansas City Southern Engine No. 103, circa 1902.*
Courtesy Noel Memorial Library Archives, LSU in Shreveport PA624: H. K. Vollrath, photographer

Union League to oppose [the secret societies], and as a result there were race riots in many sections of the state."

But military rule did end in 1877, and slowly, ever so slowly, Louisiana began to rebuild itself economically — with a major impetus from the building of the railroads. From 1880 until 1910, there was a burst of railroad building in the state that not only created employment but also created new communities wherever the rails went.

In 1860, just before the beginning of the war, Louisiana had about 300 miles of track. The war brought railroad building to a halt, and destroyed much of the track and equipment in the state. Lack of capital delayed rebuilding of the roads until the last two decades of the 1800s.

But by 1880, rails spread across the prairies of south Louisiana and began to creep through the piney hills in the north. The Texas Pacific had reached Shreveport by then, but there was a broad gap across the northern part of the state between Shreveport and Monroe, where the Vicksburg, Shreveport & Pacific had inched its way from Vicksburg and through Tallulah and Delhi. The Red River Railroad that stretched from Alexandria toward Cheneyville had been destroyed by the war and was not rebuilt. The Vidalia & Western ran the short distance from Natchez to Concordia; the West Feliciana barely got out of that parish; the Clinton & Port Hudson linked those two communities; and the Baton Rouge, Grosse Tete & and Opelousas ran only from Baton Rouge to Livonia.

The Chicago, St. Louis & New Orleans headed north out of the Crescent City and into

*Front Street, Alexandria, 1891.*
Courtesy Newcomb Camera and Art Supply, Gic Kraushaar collection.

Mississippi; the New Orleans & Carrollton and the Pontchartrain Railroad remained a local affair; the New Orleans & Mobile headed east; and the New Orleans Pacific stretched all the way to Bayougoula.

The longest continuous stretch of rails in 1880 was across south Louisiana, where Morgan's Louisiana & Texas followed the old stretch of rails that ran from Algiers to Brashear City and then on to Lafayette, where it connected with the Louisiana Western, which ran from Lafayette into Texas and ultimately made connections all the way to the Pacific Coast.

A quarter-century later, in 1915, rails criss-crossed the state. The Texas & Pacific still ran to Shreveport, but so also did the Missouri, Kansas City & Texas; the Kansas City Southern; Opelousas, Gulf & Northeastern; St. Louis

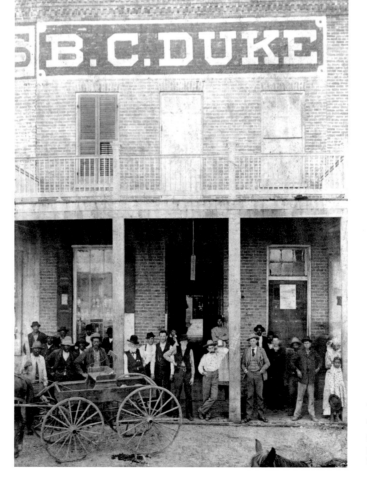

*The Brown News building housed a restaurant and railroad offices next to the depot in Lafayette, late 1800s.*

Courtesy Louis J. Perret, Clerk of Court, Lafayette Parish

*B.C. Duke's store on Front Street, Alexandria, late 1800s.*

Courtesy Newcomb Camera and Art Supply, Ellis Twilley collection

*Texas & Pacific depot at Madison and 10th Street, Alexandria.*
Courtesy Newcomb Camera and Art Supply

*West Monroe residents enjoy a Sunday outing on a railroad track built into the red hills of the community.*
Courtesy The News-Star archives

*Highwheel engine No. 170 leaving Leesville station in the early 1900s.*
Courtesy Noel Memorial Library Archives, LSU in Shreveport PA631

also a point of origin for several short lines, including the Alexandria & Western and the Tioga & Southeastern.

Morgan's Louisiana & Texas still met the Louisiana & Western at Lafayette and continued north through Opelousas to join the Texas & Pacific a few miles south of Alexandria. The New Orleans, Texas & Mexico stretched east and west from Opelousas.

And miles and miles of linking track ran from new communities such as DeRidder, which was created as the rail and milling hub for a lumber industry made possible in western Louisiana because of the rail transportation.

*Cutting cane by hand near Lafayette, circa 1890.*
Courtesy Louis J. Perret, Clerk of Court, Lafayette Parish

All across Louisiana new communities sprang up as the railroads came through. Southern Pacific put huge resources into introducing émigrés from the American Midwest to the prairies of southwest Louisiana, creating entirely new towns such as Jennings and Crowley — both of which are named for railroad men, Jennings McComb (who also ran tracks through McComb, Mississippi), and Patrick Crowley. Midwestern farmers came to the area intending to plant wheat, but they found the southwestern prairies more conducive to rice, and began planting what is now one of Louisiana's biggest crops each year.

Railroad men such as Arthur Stilwell, who stretched the Kansas City Southern south from Shreveport to Lake Charles, had huge impacts on the population and settlement patterns of the state. People moved away from the rivers that had once been the major

*Geroc's cotton gin, Lafayette, 1880.*
Courtesy Louis J. Perret, Clerk of Court, Lafayette Parish

arteries of commerce and formed new communities on the railroads. Indeed, some whole communities moved — Poupeville in what is now Acadia Parish, hitched up the church, the store, and a number of other buildings to teams of oxen and hauled them across the prairie to be next to the railroad. They named the new city Rayne, for a railroad man.

The railroads also moved Louisiana into the modern era. They offered something that we take for granted now: speed.

*Ice Plant & Bottling Works opening, Opelousas, circa 1890.*
Courtesy Opelousas Museum and Interpretive Center

*Picnic on Old River, Shreveport, circa 1895.*
Courtesy Noel Memorial Library Archives, LSU in Shreveport PB675

*Fourth of July picnic, near Opelousas, 1898. In the photo: Leonard Isaacs, Margaret Mornhinveg, Leo Lasalle, Jessie Lewis.*
Courtesy Opelousas Museum and Interpretive Center

*Bauer & Weil general merchandise store, Alexandria, circa 1895.*
Courtesy Newcomb Camera and Art Supply

*First graduating class of Louisiana State Seminary of Learning.*
Courtesy Louisiana History Museum

*Centenary sophomore class championship baseball team, Jackson, 1897.*
Courtesy Noel Memorial Library Archives, LSU in Shreveport PA601

It became possible to ship farm products to more distant but more profitable markets. Even perishable shrimp and oysters from Morgan City could be laid in ice and sold in Houston. News, goods, and the mail were now speeded from the outside world. Even the most isolated parts of Louisiana were now not nearly so alone, so far away from everything. And that included pine woodlands that had been all but ignored until the rails passed through them.

In 1880, before rails began to criss-cross Louisiana, the top three lumber producers in the United States were Michigan, Pennsylvania, and Wisconsin. Louisiana ranked thirtieth, based largely upon the cypress lumber industry that sprang up along Bayou Teche and in other parts of southern Louisiana just after the Civil War. But, those northern states were running out of harvestable timber and the cypress industry had reached its peak at about the same time Louisiana's pine forests were being opened.

Many of the northern lumbermen then moved to the pine forests of Louisiana, many of them to "cut out and get out," but some of them to stay.

The first large mill in Rapides Parish was built in 1819 by two Pennsylvanians, J. A. Bentley and E. W. Zimmerman. The mill was named for Bentley, the town that grew around it for Zimmerman. Elsewhere throughout the Louisiana pine belt in central and western

*The Lake Charles Mardi Gras festivities began in February 1895 with the arrival of the king and his retinue on the ferry Hazel. The City Market stands to the right of the ferry landing at the foot of Pujo Street.*
Courtesy McNeese State University Archives

*Alexandria Fire Station No. 2, late 1800s.*
Courtesy Louisiana History Museum

*Logging train hauling logs out of the woods near Luna, circa 1910.*
Courtesy The News Star archives

*Logging with yoked oxen around lake Charles in the late 1800s.*
Courtesy McNeese State University Archives

Louisiana, new mills and new towns sprang up like mushrooms after a rain. Mill names as often as not reflected the origins of the owners: the Hudson River Lumber Co. was far from that stream. It was in DeRidder.

Following an early map of just one rail line running south from Shreveport to Lake Charles, there are dozens of names of towns that sprang up as mill towns, many of them company towns: Larosen, Keithville, Stonewall, Keatchie, Grand Cane, Longstreet, Oxford, Trent, Catuno, Benson, Pinewood, Rosepine, Ludington, DeRidder, Bon Ami, Carson, Longville, Fulton, Gaytine, Bradley, Marion, Barnes Creek, Ramsay, Penoyer, Town Line, Camp Store,

*Monroe Lumber Company's logging camp near the turn of the century.*
Courtesy The News Star archives

*North Louisiana Lumber and Timber company employees pose by large logs being hauled by a train, circa 1900.*
Courtesy Noel Memorial Library Archives, LSU in Shreveport PB52

Old Town, Lockmoor, Lockport, and more.

Most of the first-growth pine had been cut by the 1920s, mills closed, and many of the towns around them were either shut down, if they were company towns, or simply faded away when the jobs and payrolls of the mills left the area.

*Steam locomotives on narrow gauge railways running from the lumber camps in the woods north of DeQuincy to the sawmill in Carson.*
Courtesy McNeese State University Archives

Efforts were made in the 1920s to replant some of the cut-over lands but, lack of money, lack of interest, wild hogs that ate seedlings, and fires that burned the rest slowed reforestation until the Depression-era Civilian Conservation Corps began a tree planting program.

Since then, "second-growth" forest has recovered much of the land, contributing to an industry that harvested $3.3 billion in timber in 2001, according to the Louisiana Forestry Association.

*North Louisiana Lumber and Timber company logs being transported by train, circa 1900.* Courtesy Noel Memorial Library Archives, LSU in Shreveport PB51

*A steam-operated skidder-loader helps these employees of the Central Coal and Coke Company load logs onto log cars near the sawmill town of Carson located between DeRidder and DeQuincy. The sawmill was in operation here from 1901 to 1926.* Courtesy McNeese State University Archives

## CHAPTER SIX

1901 - 1926

# Boom Days

*Spindletop is the name of a small knoll* just across the Sabine River from Louisiana near Beaumont, Texas. On January 10, 1901, Austrian-born mining engineer and former naval officer Capt. Anthony Lucas struck oil there and touched off a rash of speculation and a rush of drilling that rivaled the famous California Gold Rush.

Texas and its neighbor, Louisiana, would never be the same again.

Lucas had a theory that oil was associated with the salt domes along the Texas and Louisiana Gulf Coast. He'd asked Standard Oil, which was producing oil in Pennsylvania and elsewhere, to help finance a well to test his theory and was laughed out of the office. An executive for the nation's dominant oil company told Lucas he was crazy, he would find no oil at Spindletop.

But two Pennsylvania wildcatters, James Guffey and John Galey, took the gamble and backed Lucas' well. They began drilling on October 27, 1900.

They drilled for months without hitting pay dirt. But then, on January 10, Lucas' crew had just installed a new drilling bit and was lowering it into the 1,000-foot-deep drilling hole when the well suddenly began to spew mud, drenching the rig floor and shooting up into the derrick.

The crew ran from the rig and waited to see what would happen next. What happened was nothing. The mud geyser died out as suddenly as it started.

But then, as the crew began to clean the rig and prepare it for further drilling, they had to dash away again. More mud spewed from the hole, and then the mud quit, and it began spewing rich, black oil into the sky.

The geyser of oil gushed 200 feet or more above the sixty-foot-tall derrick — streaming out of the hole at an incredible rate of three million gallons per day. (Until Spindletop, a well that flowed at fifty barrels a day was considered a big gusher.)

By the spring of 1901, there were 200 wells on or near Spindletop knoll, and businessmen in Louisiana were beginning to take new interest in salt domes and other formations that spread along the state's coast. Captain Lucas encouraged the speculation.

In September 1901, he told a reporter for the New Orleans *Daily Picayune,* "The Louisiana region, if properly handled and developed, will yield oil in enormous quantities.

*Opposite page: The Hardie No. 2 oil well and the men who brought it in, circa 1919.*
Courtesy Noel Memorial Library Archives, LSU in Shreveport PB249: Sims Linderman photo

*W.P. Stiles No. 107, circa 1910.*

… Two years ago, when I was working in Louisiana, I brought in the Anse La Butte well [near Breaux Bridge in southern Louisiana], but it did not yield oil in paying quantities. Those who owned the property would not let me go deep enough, and I accordingly went over to Beaumont and eventually brought in the famous gusher. The Texas region is not better than Louisiana. In fact, I believe the latter is superior to the former. The oil I drew at Anse La Butte is certainly of a higher grade than the Texas oil and in some respects better than any oil in the United States."

That pronouncement and others were all that was needed. The first well in Louisiana, the Jules Clement No. 1, was brought in on September 21, 1901, near Jennings by W. Scott Heywood and a group of local investors. That well filled with sand and quit producing, but others were drilled nearby and by 1903 the Evangeline Oil Field in south Louisiana was in business.

In later years, south Louisiana and the adjacent Gulf of Mexico would again be the focus of the oil industry. But in the early 1900s, a north Louisiana field stole the thunder.

Development of the Caddo Oil Field began in 1902, when Ellison Adger of Belcher decided to drill an artesian water well. He struck salt water at 400 feet and stopped drilling. He sent a core sample to government scientists, asking them if there was a possibility that he could continue to drill and find fresh water beneath the salt.

*Early oil well Anse La Butte field in Louisiana, 1908.*

The scientists reported back that he wasn't likely to strike fresh water, but he would hit oil and gas. Adger wanted water. He abandoned the well.

Down the road, however, the Kansas City Southern Railroad had drilled a twenty-foot

well and found water. As the story goes, a passing hobo dropped a lighted match into the well, and gas fumes exploded into a ball of fire. He told his story to a storekeeper named S. H. Nunnely, who figured out what was going on.

Nunnely and a partner, S. C. Richardson, bought and leased as much land as they could in the area, and began drilling. They found oil, but not enough of it. They gave up their well, but not before others began to take interest in the Caddo region. By the middle 1900s, literally hundreds of wells were producing thousands of barrels of oil in the Caddo field.

In 1913, the Bull Bayou Field turned into a major producer in northwest Louisiana and in 1916 drillers brought in the Monroe Gas Field, another huge field. By 1926 the state boasted thirty fields producing more than 23 million barrels of oil each year and 150 billion cubic feet of natural gas.

The successes in these early oil fields led to speculation all across the state, and eventually commercial quantities of oil were found in fifty-four of the state's sixty-four parishes, and oil royalties and fees became the basis not only of huge personal fortunes, but also of the state's economy. By the early 1980s, fully half of all revenue going to the Louisiana government came from taxes on oil operations, gasoline taxes, oil royalties, and oil leases.

As the oil and gas fields were developed, a modern petrochemical industry began to develop alongside at Baton Rouge, Monroe, Shreveport, and Lake Charles, partially because

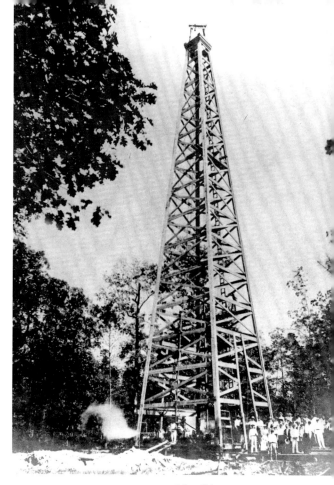

*Oil well known as Spyker #1, owned by Progressive Oil and Gas Company, northeast Louisiana, 1916.*
Courtesy News-Star archives

*Union Oil Mill, circa 1920. This is the oldest company in Ouachita Parish, founded in 1883 by L. D. McLain.*
Courtesy The News-Star archives

*Scene on bayou near Stacey's Landing.* Courtesy Noel Memorial Library Archives, LSU in Shreveport PB247: Sims Linderman photo

of the abundance of raw materials, but also because of Louisiana's miles and miles of deep navigable waterways available to tankers and used to supply the water for the petrochemical process.

Since then, inland production has declined, but advanced technology has enabled oilmen to drill in thousands of feet of water in the Gulf of Mexico off the Louisiana shore to produce millions of barrels of oil and trillions of cubic feet of natural gas.

Oddly enough, the birth of the offshore industry can be found in the piney woods of north Louisiana. In 1907, driller J. P. McCann sank a well in about twelve feet of water in Caddo Lake.

The first offshore well in the Gulf of Mexico was completed in 12 feet of water about 300 feet off the coast of Cameron Parish, and in 1937 a well was completed more than a mile from the coast by the Pure and Superior oil companies. But the offshore industry was officially born in 1947, when the Kerr-McGee Oil Company completed the first well out of the sight of land in the Gulf of Mexico off Terrebonne Parish.

Oil lease and royalty income going to the state peaked in 1982 at $624,529,812, and dropped to only a third of that in 1999 at $237,967,797. In those same years, oil and gas severance taxes totaled $971,677,140 and $354,765,574.

Oil not only brought dollars, it brought a wave of speculators, drillers, financiers, and freeloaders. In the 1900 Census, taken before the wave of oil speculation in the Shreveport area, the population of the town was 16,013. Ten years later, it had nearly doubled to 28,015. It continued at that pace, to 43,874 in 1920, 76,655 in 1930, and 98,167 in 1940.

The boom came later for Lafayette. There was no huge oil field in the parish, so it capitalized on location. In 1952, merchant, real estate investor, and entrepreneur Maurice Heymann began construction on the first buildings of an Oil Center to provide office space for exploration and development companies. His first proposal was for about 100,000 square feet of office space to house a dozen or so companies. By the 1980s, when Louisiana oil activity reached its peak, the Heymann Oil Center included more than a million square feet of office and retail space and housed some 700 oil-related companies.

That center changed the face of Lafayette. The population jumped from 33,541 in 1950 to 40,400 in 1960 and then took off like a rocket, to 68,908 in 1970, and 81,961 in 1980. Even after a period of decline as the oil industry suffered through hard times in the middle 1980s, Lafayette's population growth continued.

As the industry began to move farther into the Gulf of Mexico, other south Louisiana communities such as Houma, Morgan City, and New Iberia began to grow and prosper as bases for the offshore industry. Fabrication yards at places such as the Port of Iberia and at Amelia created thousands of jobs as they welded the towering platforms that would be towed into the Gulf of Mexico.

The largest workman's navy in the world began to operate out of Louisiana bases to haul men and supplies to these rigs; Petroleum Helicopters Inc. developed the largest civilian helicopter fleet in the world to do the same thing.

*Louisiana Purchase: A Pictorial Retrospective Celebrating Louisiana*

**Left:** *Knights of Columbus State Convention held in Opelousas in the early 1900s.*

Courtesy Opelousas Museum and Interpretive Center

**Below:** *Law offices of E.B. Herndon, Sr., and E.B. Herndon, Jr., Shreveport, circa 1900.*

Courtesy Noel Memorial Library Archives, LSU in Shreveport PC1190

Left: *Pupils and the "transfer" in front of the first Youngsville School, early 1900s.*
Courtesy Louis J. Perret,
Clerk of Court, Lafayette Parish

Right: *Second Street, looking north, Alexandria, circa 1900.*
Courtesy Newcomb Camera and Art Supply,
Leon Diagre, Sr. collection

Below: *Downtown Baton Rouge in the early 1900s.*
Courtesy Louisiana State Archives, Lindee Collection

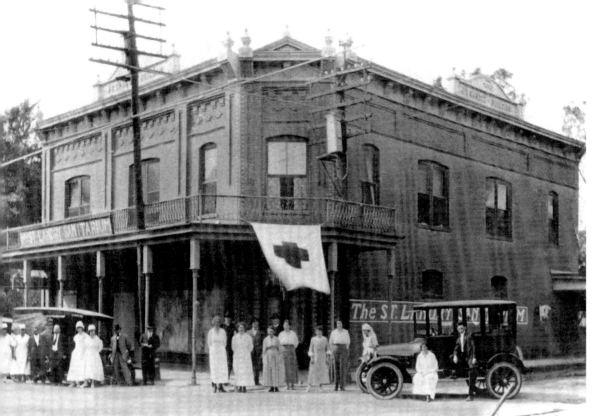

**Left:** *St. Landry Sanitarium on Main and Grolee Street, Opelousas, circa 1900.*
Courtesy Opelousas Museum
and Interpretive Center

**Below:** *Courthouse, Caddo Parish, circa 1900.*
Courtesy Noel Memorial Library
Archives, LSU in Shreveport PC13

*Boom Days*

**Above:** *Confederates on horseback. These eight Confederates met years after the Civil War at a reunion at Chargois Springs, near the present American Legion Hall.*

Courtesy Louis J. Perret, Clerk of Court, Lafayette Parish

**Left:** *Columbia Theatre on Third Street in Baton Rouge, early 1900s.*

Courtesy Louisiana State Archives, Lindee Collection

**Below:** *Interior of a local business, Opelousas, early 1900s.* Courtesy Opelousas Museum and Interpretive Center

Right: *SLI (UL) football team, 1903.*

Below: *SLII Baseball Team, circa 1900.*

*Boom Days*

**Left:** *Moss Pharmacy, Lafayette, 1906.*
Courtesy Louis J. Perret, Clerk of Court, Lafayette Parish

**Below:** *St. Francis Xavier Convent School children, circa 1905.* Courtesy Newcomb Camera and Art Supply, Ellis Twilley Collection

**Above:** *Main Street, Pollock, circa 1906.*
Courtesy Newcomb Camera and Art Supply, Dorothy W. Till Collection

**Below:** *Ball Hotel on Front Street, Pollock, circa 1905.*
Courtesy Newcomb Camera and Art Supply, Dorothy W. Till Collection

**Left:** *Pinkies Sorority at Louisiana Industrial Institute in Ruston, circa 1907.* Courtesy The News-Star archives

**Below:** *Shreveport police force, 1917.*
Courtesy Noel Memorial Library Archives,
LSU in Shreveport PD163

**Above:** *Bernstein family out for a drive around Shreveport in their new automobile, Shreveport, 1909.*
Courtesy Noel Memorial Library Archives, LSU in Shreveport  PA3968

**Right:** *W.K. Henderson Iron Works employees, Shreveport, 1908.*  Courtesy Noel Memorial Library Archives, LSU in Shreveport  PA3112

**Left:** *St. Landry Catholic Church, Opelousas, 1910. The building was constructed in 1908.*
Courtesy Opelousas Museum and Interpretive Center

**Below:** *Overton home, 8th at Washington, Alexandria, circa 1910.*
Courtesy Newcomb Camera and
Art Supply, Herbie Mount collection

**Above:** *Daniel Lumber Company employees, Opelousas, circa 1910.* Courtesy Opelousas Museum and Interpretive Center

**Left:** *Employees of the Peoples State Bank, Opelousas, circa 1910.* Courtesy Opelousas Museum and Interpretive Center

**Above:** *Interior of J.P. Sandoz General Merchandise Store, Opelousas, circa 1910.*
Courtesy Opelousas Museum and Interpretive Center

**Left:** *Gondoor Joseph's store, Lafayette, 1910.*
Courtesy Louis J. Perret, Clerk of Court, Lafayette Parish

**Right:** *High school graduating class, Opelousas, 1914.* Courtesy Opelousas Museum and Interpretive Center

**Above:** *Centenary College Football Team, 1912–1913. Left to right, back row: Truman Wilbanks, Earl (Dick) Whittington, McVae Higginbotham, Perry Brown, fullback; Paul Brown, quarterback; unidentified. Bottom row: unidentified, I.B. Robertson, T.J. Rogers, Ellis H. Brown, center; unidentifed, unidentified, unidentified.*
Courtesy Noel Memorial Library Archives, LSU in Shreveport PD124

**Right:** *R.H. McFaddin's store, Lafayette.* Courtesy Louis J. Perret, Clerk of Court, Lafayette Parish

**Below:** *Mardi Gras Carnival parade, Shreveport, 1912.*
Courtesy Noel Memorial Library Archives, LSU in Shreveport PC1184

**Above:** *Sitting in a vintage Maxwell are: Mrs. H.L Ducrocq, Flossie Montgomery, and Elsie Shakerford. Dr. Felix Girard is at the wheel, circa 1915.* Courtesy Louis J. Perret, Clerk of Court, Lafayette Parish

**Above:** *Fire Station No. 1 on Fifth Street, Alexandria, circa 1915.*
Courtesy Newcomb Camera and Art Supply, Alexandria Historical and Genealogical Library and Museum

**Right:** *Bolton High School basketball team on Beauregard Street, circa 1915.*
Courtesy Newcomb Camera and Art Supply, Bolton High School collection

**Below:** *Monroe postal workers, circa 1915.*
Courtesy Ouachita Parish Public Library, Special Archives Collection

Above: *Cotton ginning in Colfax, circa 1915. This was later the location of Central Wholesale Grocery Company.* Courtesy Newcomb Camera and Art Supply, T.H. McNelly Estate Collection

Above: *St. Landry Lumber Company on North Railroad Avenue, Opelousas, circa 1915.* Courtesy Opelousas Museum and Interpretive Center

Left: *Fairmont School, "Kateland," South of Colfax, circa 1915.*
Courtesy Newcomb Camera and Art Supply

Below: *Central Louisiana Motor Company, Alexandria. Mrs. W. Lennie-Smith, Proprietor and manager, circa 1915.*
Courtesy Newcomb Camera and Art Supply, Neil Daspit Collection

**Above:** *Clary's grocery store on Main Street, Opelousas, circa 1915.*
Courtesy Opelousas Museum and Interpretive Center

**Left:** *Monroe City Hall, circa 1915, was built with funds generated through a tax passed in 1904.* Courtesy The News-Star archives

**Right:** *Sheriff Marion Swords' funeral procession, Opelousas, 1916. He was shot to death by Hilaire Carrier on July 17, 1916. Carrier was hanged on October 19, 1917 at the St. Landry Parish Courthouse Square.*
Courtesy Opelousas Museum and Interpretive Center

**Above:** *The first truck in Monroe was this REO bought by the Coca-Cola Co. in 1914. John Gernon is the driver.*

**Left:** *An Independence Day parade in Lafayette observed from the gallery of the Union Hotel at left.*
Courtesy Louis J. Perret, Clerk of Court, Lafayette Parish

**Right:** *Interior of the planing mill, Allen Manufacturing Company, Shreveport, 1918.*

Courtesy Noel Memorial Library Archives, LSU in Shreveport PA169

**Below:** *"Bat" Comus and A.L. Domingue pose with other crew members in front of Southern Pacific steam engine.*

Courtesy Louis J. Perret, Clerk of Court, Lafayette Parish

Above: *Weighing and packing department,*
*Cuban Coffee Mills, Shreveport, 1918.*
Courtesy Noel Memorial Library Archives, LSU in Shreveport PA236

Above: *Iron workers,*
*W. K. Henderson Iron Works,*
*Shreveport, 1918.*
Courtesy Noel Memorial Library Archives,
LSU in Shreveport PA199

Right: *Auto service department,*
*Crawford-Jenkins-*
*Booth Company Limited,*
*Shreveport, 1918.*
Courtesy Noel Memorial Library Archives,
LSU in Shreveport PA283

Below: *Elliott Electric*
*Company, Shreveport, 1918.*
Courtesy Noel Memorial Library Archives,
LSU in Shreveport PA224

Below: *Interior of Crescent Cash store, Shreveport,*
*1918.* Courtesy Noel Memorial Library Archives, LSU in Shreveport PA372

Above: *Gerstner Field, one of the largest of the World War I pilot training fields in the United States, was constructed in 1917 southeast of Lake Charles. Cadets trained in open cockpit Curtiss JN-4's and Thomas Morse SB-4's before being sent overseas. Four of these pilots stand in front of their Curtiss JN-4. First on the left is Herman C. Krause; third from the left is Roy French.*
Courtesy McNeese State University Archives, Gerstner Field Collection

Above: *Group of people celebrate the end of World War I, Shreveport, 1918.*
Courtesy Noel Memorial Library Archives, LSU in Shreveport PD123

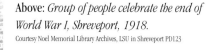

Left: *The nation's third Liberty Loan Day was observed in downtown Lake Charles on April 27, 1918. Gerstner Field furnished troops to march in the parade as well as pilots flying in formation above the city. Over $3 billion dollars was raised nationwide during this third campaign to aid the war effort.*
Murrey Photograph, Courtesy McNeese State University Archives, Gerstner Field Collection

Below: *Railroad yard close to depot, Pollock, circa 1920. "Uncle Doc" Granger is in the wagon on the left.*
Courtesy Newcomb Camera and Art Supply, Sharon Granger Braxton Collection

**Above:** *Round stable on the corner of Court and Vine streets in Opelousas, built by the late Dr. John Haas. It was built before 1900 and was demolished by the Haas estate in the 1930s.*
Courtesy Opelousas Museum and Interpretive Center

**Above:** *Market Days, Colfax, circa 1920.*
Courtesy Newcomb Camera and Art Supply, T.H. McNeely Estate Collection

**Left:** *Jefferson Street, downtown Lafayette, 1920s.*
Courtesy Louis J. Perret, Clerk of Court, Lafayette Parish

**Below:** *Suffragette meeting at the capitol grounds in Baton Rouge, June 20, 1920.*
Courtesy Noel Memorial Library Archives, LSU in Shreveport PC1319

**Above:** *Minden High School girls'*
*basketball team, 1921.*
Courtesy Noel Memorial Library Archives,
LSU in Shreveport PA2394: Grabill Studio photo

**Above:** *Centenary College football team, Shreveport,*
*1921.* Courtesy Noel Memorial Library Archives, LSU in Shreveport PC1313

**Left:** *First service station in Pollock, early 1920s.*
*Earnest M. Granger on the left, next to him is James*
*H. "Uncle Doc" Granger. Others unknown.*
Courtesy Newcomb Camera and Art Supply, Sharon Granger Braxton Collection

**Below:** *St. Paul's Elementary School graduates of*
*1923, Lafayette. Standing: Kermit Patty, Gabriel*
*Jacquet, Jr., Felix Mouton, Victor Broussard, Zoe*
*Marie LeBlanc, Robert Green, Eary Jacquet. Sitting:*
*Roberta Elizabeth Johnson, Ophella Jones, Zola*
*Amond, Gertrude Claiborne, Martha Brown.*
Courtesy Louis J. Perret, Clerk of Court, Lafayette Parish

**Above:** *Jurors in the Bobby Dunbar case, Opelousas, 1922.*
Courtesy Opelousas Museum and Interpretive Center

**Above:** *Civil War Veterans Reunion on the steps of the Old Court House, Alexandria, October 12, 1923.*
Courtesy Newcomb Camera and Art Supply,
Mrs. Walter Price Collection

**Left:** *Rosenthal High School girls basketball team, Alexandria, 1923. Ruth Beasley was the coach.*
Courtesy Newcomb Camera and Art Supply

**Below:** *Texas Street at Market looking west toward First Methodist Church, Shreveport, 1923.*
Courtesy Noel Memorial Library Archives, LSU in Shreveport:
Grabill Studio photo

Above: *Central Fire Station, Shreveport, 1920s.* Courtesy Noel Memorial Library Archives, LSU in Shreveport PC1083: Grabill Studio photo

Above: *Western Union messenger, Willie J. Monreau, Opelousas, circa 1925.* Courtesy Opelousas Museum and Interpretive Center

Left: *Lafayette Rotary boys band, early 1920s.*
Courtesy Louis J. Perret, Clerk of Court, Lafayette Parish

Below: *Cotton Exchange between Murray and Johnston on Fourth Street, Alexandria, circa 1926.*
Courtesy Newcomb Camera and Art Supply,
E. Otis Edgerton Jr. Collection

**Right:** *Theo's Grocery at 607 Texas Street, Shreveport, circa 1925. John K. Theo was the proprietor.*
Courtesy Noel Memorial Library Archives, LSU in Shreveport PA2882

**Below:** *Interior of Luke Martin store, Lafayette, 1926.*
Courtesy Louis J. Perret, Clerk of Court, Lafayette Parish

**Above:** *Flood of 1927 in Melville.*
Courtesy Opelousas Museum and Interpretive Center

**Left:** *Tent city set up during the 1927 flood in Lafayette.*
Courtesy Louis J. Perret, Clerk of Court, Lafayette Parish

**Below:** *West Monroe during the flood of 1927.* Courtesy The News-Star archives

**Above:** *Downtown Melville during the flood of 1927.*
Courtesy Opelousas Museum and Interpretive Center

## CHAPTER SEVEN

1928 - 1939

# The Long Era

*If the money flowing* from oil and gas fields changed the economy of Louisiana in the middle 1900s, there was another force, perhaps equally powerful, that changed practically everything else. His name was Huey Pierce Long.

The question of whether the sweeping changes inaugurated during his days of power — and the ways that they were accomplished — were for good or for ill still kindles heated debate. There is one certainty: Everyone who knew him or knows of him has an opinion.

Historians have described him variously as Louisiana's greatest humanitarian, as a "tinpot Napoleon," as a political genius, as saint and as sinner, and by John K. Fineran, who minced no words, as "that most extraordinary mountebank, that most mendacious liar, that eminent blackguard and distinguished sneak-thief."

As a young man, Long planned to study for the ministry but instead became a lawyer. He apparently was always interested in politics. He ran for the state railroad commission at the tender age of twenty-four with a populist campaign that would become his trademark — urging the "little man" to elect him to stand up against the "big corporations" and protect the people's rights. He beat the incumbent by 658 votes in that campaign and immediately began to follow his campaign promise and to take on the giant Standard Oil.

In 1922, Long became president of the Public Service Commission, which had replaced the Railroad Commission, and involved himself in fights to lower streetcar rates in Shreveport and telephone rates in all of Louisiana. He tried out his "poor man" political philosophy in the 1924 gubernatorial election and pulled in a large rural vote, but not enough to win the election. He did learn valuable political lessons, however, and the outcome was far different in 1928, when he received 40,000 votes more than his nearest rival.

In his first days in the governor's chair, Long began the tactics that made him hero or devil, depending upon whether or not you were in his favor. Political opponents at every level of government found themselves out of work, replaced by Long supporters. Legislators

*Huey Pierce Long.*
Courtesy Library of Congress

**Opposite page:** *The old state capitol building during a rare snow storm.*
Courtesy Louisiana State Archives

who did not support him got no money for public works projects in their districts.

As one history reports, "Long virtually forced people to be for him. There was no middle ground. As his position became stronger, he began to deliver on his campaign promises. Long was certainly unlike the traditional demagogue who promised much before election day and delivered nothing after the votes were counted. Huey Long kept his promises."

He provided free textbooks for Louisiana schools, built roads, put the first bridges across the Mississippi River, had a building inspector condemn the governor's mansion so that he could tear it down and build a fancier one, and — remembering his old nemesis, Standard Oil — called a special session of the legislature to put a five-cents-a-barrel tax on oil refined in Louisiana. (Standard had the only refinery in the state at the time.)

Standard Oil fought back, and enlisted the support of major newspapers and others who did not like Long's methods — including enough members of the Louisiana legislature to impeach him. Long appealed to the "little people," telling them the issue was between rule by the people and rule by the mighty. His backers from rural Louisiana flocked to Baton Rouge for what the *Abbeville Meridional* called "a mighty demonstration protesting the injustice and persecution being visited on Governor Huey P. Long by the votaries of Greed and Graft."

But he did not rely just on his "little people" friends. He also squeezed the members of the Louisiana senate who were to decide the matter — hard enough that fifteen of them signed a "Round Robin" petition pledging that there were no circumstances that would make them vote to oust the governor.

*In 1918, the first effort to create an east-to-west-coast highway began in Columbus, Georgia. The road was named the Dixie-Overland Highway, now U.S. Highway 80. After 1928, Louisiana's governor, Huey P. Long, included the Louisiana portion in his highway projects. Cutting the ribbon at the dedication of the Long administration's first section are from left: Volney Voss Whittington, state representative from Bossier Parish Parish from 1928 to 1932; Robert Brother, Shreveport; Governor and Mrs. Long; J.R. Wendt, state maintenance engineer (formerly Bossier Parish Engineer, responsible for planting live oak and magnolia trees along Highway 190 outside Baton Rouge); J.G. McDade, president of the Bossier Parish Police Jury; V.R. Rucher, and two unidentified participants.* Courtesy Noel Memorial Library Archives, LSU in Shreveport PC1940

Emboldened, he ran for the U.S. Senate, won the election, and announced that he would not give up his seat as governor until his term expired. He was too busy with his plans for a new state capitol, expanded highways, a Mississippi River bridge at New Orleans, and expansion at his beloved Louisiana State University to move to Washington right away. He did not take his seat in the Senate until two years after his election. Lt. Gov. Paul M. Cyr argued that Long could not hold two offices at once, and had himself sworn in as governor. When he tried to move into the governor's office, he found the National Guard blocking his way. Long then turned the tables, announcing that since Cyr had taken the oath as governor, he must have given up the job of lieutenant governor. He appointed another, more faithful lieutenant. Cyr went to court. The court ruled for Huey.

Even before he went to Washington, signs urging "Huey Long for President" began to appear in Louisiana. When he finally got to the nation's capital, Huey began to think that might be a good idea. He went to Washington as a strong supporter of Franklin D. Roosevelt and his New Deal to handle the Depression that had swept the nation by those times. But Huey soon began to develop his own "Share the Wealth" program that he thought better than the New Deal.

*The state capitol building in Baton Rouge is the tallest in the nation at 450 feet and 34 floors.*
Courtesy Louisiana Office of Tourism

His plan would, among other things, take money away from the very rich and give up to $5,000 to every family in the United States to use to buy a home, car, and radio. It provided a minimum annual wage, an old-age pension, set a shorter work week, and subsidized some farm programs. His program, his slogan said, would make "Every Man a King."

Roosevelt was beginning to regard Long as a serious opponent by 1935 when, on September 8, the Louisiana populist was fatally shot as he walked through his new skyscraper state capitol.

Huey Long's death changed Louisiana as much as his life did. Only he could control the huge political machine that he had created, and when he died it continued to run, but to run out of control. Huey's chief lieutenants, foremost among them his brother Earl, tried to grab the reins, but none could command the entire machine as Huey had done.

In the 1936 gubernatorial election, each of the pretenders to Huey's empty throne saw that they could not win, and each of them wanted to be sure that none of the other strong leaders won the election. As much for self-protection as anything else, they came together to back a relatively obscure New Orleans judge, Richard W. Leche, for governor. Earl ran for lieutenant governor to keep the Long name on the ballot.

Leche won and was sworn to office. But, as he remarked some time later, "When I took the oath of office, I didn't take any vows of poverty."

Some historians estimate that as much as $100 million in state funds disappeared while Leche was governor. Not all of it went to Leche himself. Louisiana State University president James Monroe Smith ran off with a half million dollars after having run through another half million gambling on the stock market.

But it came to an end in 1939, when federal investigators secured 250 indictments against 51 people and 17 business firms, including income tax evasion, mail fraud, oil regulation violations, fraud, conspiracy, and just about everything else in the criminal code short of murder. Leche was forced to resign. Smith fled to Canada, then returned for trial. Investigators looked long and hard at Earl Long but could find nothing on him. He became governor, but only for a short while.

The 1940 election pitted pro-Long versus anti-Long opponents at every level of government, and the so-called Reform Ticket was swept into office on the coattails of Lake Charles lawyer Sam Jones, who defeated Earl for governor.

In 1942, Jimmie H. Davis became public service commissioner, the same job that Huey Long had once held. Two years later he was elected governor. Best known for composing the song, "You Are My Sunshine," Davis served as governor for two terms (1944-1948 and 1960-1964), all the while continuing his musical career.

By 1948, Louisiana was ready for a do-something governor, and turned once again to the Long family. "Uncle Earl" moved from his "Peapatch Farm" to the governor's mansion, beginning another colorful, turbulent, but also productive era of Louisiana politics.

*Mitchell's Musical Miniatures, Shreveport, 1928.*

Courtesy Noel Memorial Library Archives, LSU in Shreveport PC528

**Above:** *School bus drivers in front of Boyce High School, Alexandria, 1928.*
Courtesy Newcomb Camera and Art Supply, Francia A. Rougeou collection

**Left:** *City Council, Pineville, 1928. Left to right, back row: H. Jewell Daigre, Joe Miller, R.D. Lofton, Lamar Polk, John Woodward, Grady David, Courtney VonSenden. Front row: Rollo Lawrence, W.D. "Willie" Dannenburg, C.C. Coats, J.M. "Matt" Rembert (Mayor), J.R. Tullos, J.T. Ball.*
Courtesy Newcomb Camera and Art Supply, James A. Gabour collection

**Below:** *Interior of Palace Café, Opelousas, circa 1929. Note the slot machine on the counter in the foreground.*
Courtesy Opelousas Museum and Interpretive Center

**Above:** *Belcher Gin Company, Belcher, 1928.*

Courtesy Noel Memorial Library Archives, LSU in Shreveport PB4

**Above:** *Crystal Oil Refining Corporation, Shreveport, circa 1930.*

Courtesy Noel Memorial Library Archives, LSU in Shreveport PC1115: Grabill Studio photo

**Left:** *Louisiana Oil Refining Corporation at the corner of Stoner and Market, Shreveport, circa 1930.*

Courtesy Noel Memorial Library Archives, LSU in Shreveport PC2085

**Above:** *State, city and parish law enforcement officers, Lafayette, 1930. Front row: John LeBlanc and Cas Chargois. Second row: unidentified state police officers. Third row: "Gaboon" Trahan, John Gallagher, Dan Roy, Lawrence (Larry) Logan, Malcolm Fisher, John Tujaque, Mr. De Blanc, Alphonse Peck, Frank E. Moss, Adam Mouton and "Shorty" Ledel Sonnier.* Courtesy Louis J. Perret, Clerk of Court, Lafayette Parish

Left: *St. Francis Xavier girl's basketball team, Alexandria, 1931. Elizabeth Lawrence Baumann is the fourth from left, back row.*
Courtesy Newcomb Camera and Art Supply, George Baumann collection

Below: *Construction of the Texas Street Bridge, Shreveport, 1931. This view is looking east toward Bossier City.*
Courtesy Noel Memorial Library Archives, LSU in Shreveport PC1719: Grabill Studio photo

**Right:** *Raoul "Cow" Landry is shown in 1938 with some of the trophies he won in track competition during his time at SLI (UL) from 1934 to 1937. He also ran in the 1936 Olympic trials. In addition to his track accomplishments, Landry also lettered in football and basketball as an all-around athlete.*
Courtesy Louis J. Perret, Clerk of Court, Lafayette Parish

**Below:** *Tioga High School basketball team, 1931.*
Courtesy Newcomb Camera and
Art Supply, Marvin Gore Collection

**Above:** *Flooding in Monroe, January 20, 1932.*
Courtesy Ouachita Parish Public Library, Special Archives Collection

**Left and below:** *Flooding in West Monroe, February 1932.*
Courtesy Ouachita Parish Public Library, Special Archives Collection

**Right:** *Bishop Cornelius Van De Van's funeral, Fourth Street in front of St. Francis Xavier Cathedral, Alexandria, May 8, 1932.*
Courtesy Newcomb Camera and Art Supply, John Kramer and Son Funeral Home Collection

**Below:** *Flooding in Alexandria, circa 1932.*
Courtesy Newcomb Camera and Art Supply, Margaret Todd Collection

AIR-PORT

RAPIDES FISH MARKET 1s

**Above:** *Line Avenue Mardi Gras, Shreveport, 1934. Court, left to right: Ruth Gray Knighton, Sally Ann, Bill Harwell, unidentified princess, Betty Sue Snyder, Queen; Camp Flournoy, King; unidentified prince, Lewis Carter, Louise Manning and Jack Holloway.* Courtesy Noel Memorial Library Archives, LSU in Shreveport PC1871

**Right:** *Johnnie Morris, hurdler, Lafayette, 1933.* Courtesy Louis J. Perret, Clerk of Court, Lafayette Parish

**Below:** *P. Krauss Jewelers in Lafayette, circa 1933.* Courtesy Louis J. Perret, Clerk of Court, Lafayette Parish

*The Long Era*

**Right:** *The first lot of air mail sent out of Monroe, 1934.*
Courtesy The News-Star archives

**Below:** *George Gardiner on his Mardi Gras float serving as Lafayette's first King Gabriel.*
Courtesy Louis J. Perret, Clerk of Court, Lafayette Parish

**Above:** *Vermilion Barber Shop, Lafayette, 1930s. Barbers, from left, are O.J. "Slim" LeBlanc, Ulysses Arceneaux and Placid Cormier. In the chairs are Louis Arceneaux and A. Cormier. The shoeshine man is Mr. Washington.* Courtesy Louis J. Perret, Clerk of Court, Lafayette Parish

**Left:** *Dr. M.E. Dodd, pastor of the First Baptist Church, Shreveport, circa 1935.*

Courtesy Noel Memorial Library Archives, LSU in Shreveport PC1152: Milburne's Studio photo

**Below:** *The interior of Bulleaud's General Store, Lafayette, as it appeared in the 1930s. It was located on Jefferson Street.* Courtesy Louis J. Perret, Clerk of Court, Lafayette Parish

**Left:** *Barksdale Army Air Field floats for Shreveport's Centennial, June 29, 1935.*
U. S. Army Air Corps photo courtesy Noel Memorial Library Archives,
LSU in Shreveport PC872

**Below:** *School bus for the Ouachita Parish Junior College in the 1930s. The school, which opened in 1931, later became University of Louisiana at Monroe.*
Courtesy The News-Star archives

**Above:** *Delivering sugar cane to the mill by mule wagon in Lafayette Parish, 1930s.*
Courtesy Louis J. Perret, Clerk of Court, Lafayette Parish

**Below:** *Alexandria fire department and merchants.*
Courtesy Newcomb Camera and Art Supply, Joseph Sitton collection

**Left:** *Barksdale Army Air Field, Shreveport, circa 1935.*
Courtesy Noel Memorial Library
Archives, LSU in Shreveport PC876

**Right:** *Cathedral High School basketball team, Lafayette, 1936. Front row: George Benard, Francis Guidroz, C. J. Aillet, Odo Blanchet, Louis Estilette; Back row: Lucere Dore, Charles Trahan, Vernon Mouton, Brother Bernard.*

Courtesy Louis J. Perret, Clerk of Court, Lafayette Parish

**Below:** *Strand Theatre, May 26, 1936, Shreveport.*

Courtesy Noel Memorial Library Archives, LSU in Shreveport PC905: LeDoux's photo

**Above:** *Bergeron's Gulf Station at the corner of Fifth and Murray, Alexandria, circa 1937.*
Courtesy Newcomb Camera and
Art Supply, Leon Bergeron Collection

**Left:** *Labor Day parade in downtown Shreveport, circa 1937. Carrying the flag is John Russell Torrano. Carrying the banner is Russell G. Torrano. The little boy in front is Michael E. Torrano.*
Courtesy Noel Memorial Library Archives,
LSU in Shreveport PC1175

*Right:* *Boy Scout Troop No. 12 clothing collection, Alexandria, circa 1938.*
Courtesy Newcomb Camera and Art Supply,
Leon Bergeron family Collection

*Below:* *Alexandria Business College students, circa 1937.*
Courtesy Newcomb Camera and Art Supply,
Mrs. R.R. Brasher Collection

Above: *New Cedar Grove Line trolley, Shreveport, December 1939. This was the last to be converted from a street car.* Courtesy Noel Memorial Library Archives, LSU in Shreveport PC1258

Left: *Children's Carnival in 1937, Jerry Andrus Arceneaux was Queen Titania and N.J. Primeaux was King Oberon in Lafayette Childrens Carnival. Jerry Arceneaux later became Chief of Police in Carencro.* Courtesy Louis J. Perret, Clerk of Court, Lafayette Parish

Below: *Texas Street, 700 block, Shreveport, 1939.* Courtesy Noel Memorial Library Archives, LSU in Shreveport PA2852

Next page: *Milam Street, 700 block, Shreveport, circa 1945.*
Courtesy Noel Memorial Library Archives, LSU in Shreveport PC2069: Grabill Studio photo

THE COMMANDOS OF MAIN STREET!
THEY'RE OFF FOR THE $500,000.00
VICTORY QUOTA
IN WAR BONDS AND STAMPS ·· IN THE
" RETAILERS FOR VICTORY "
NATIONWIDE CAMPAIGN!

## CHAPTER EIGHT

1940 - 1949

# World War II

*In the summer of 1941,* Gen. George S. Patton did what Gen. Nathaniel Banks failed to do three-quarters of a century before: He captured Shreveport.

His "attack" on the city was part of the largest dress rehearsal in United States military history, a series of "war games" designed to prepare the army for battle in World War II.

Four months before Pearl Harbor, the nation was not yet at war, but it was becoming increasingly apparent to military planners that there was a very good chance that U.S. troops would have to fight in Europe, and it was equally apparent that they were not ready to do so. When the war erupted in Europe, the United States was far from the Superpower it is today. The American army still used World War I vintage weapons. There were more cavalry horses than tanks. Every military force was undermanned, undertrained, and poorly led.

The Great Louisiana Maneuvers were designed at first to sort out good officers from bad, test tactics, expose enlisted men to the realities of war, and to generally rate the effectiveness, or lack of it, of the army.

To do this, the Army selected a 3,400-square-mile area of central and western Louisiana and east Texas, for a huge training exercise that would pit the Red Army against the Blue Army. Camp Beauregard, which had been built in 1917 in Pineville to train National Guard units, became U.S. 3<sup>rd</sup> Army Headquarters, and construction began on several new bases to accommodate a huge influx of troops into the area.

Camp Polk was constructed in Leesville at that time and has since become Fort Polk. During World War II it became the largest armored force training camp in the United States. Camp Claiborne, just north of Forest Hill in central Louisiana, remained open as a training base for more than a half million soldiers during World War II, but was shut down just after the war. Camp Livingston near Tioga served as a training camp for more than 14,000 troops during World War II. Now a part of the Kisatchie National Forest, this camp also held German and Italian POWs after the war.

In purely economic terms, the nation's entry into the war could be considered a blessing, as defense spending helped bring about a recovery from the Great Depression. The rural South was a prime beneficiary of that spending.

According to Jerry Purvis Sanson's survey of Louisiana during the war years, "During World War II, the South received some $4,442,000 in federal funds for war plants, 17.6 percent of the national total. Louisiana received more of these funds than any other state except Texas — about $1,773,713,000. … Higgins Industries alone made New Orleans an

*Opposite page: War Bond drive in Shreveport, 1940s.*
Courtesy Noel Memorial Library Archives, LSU in Shreveport

*Camp Beauregard,
circa 1940.*

important manufacturing center, while smaller enterprises produced myriad goods for the war effort. Baton Rouge became one of the most important oil refining centers in the United States. Shreveport played a role in supplying goods produced in plants in the city and also hosted troops in training, while nearby Bossier City was the site of Barksdale Army Air Field. Lake Charles provided oil products, training facilities and a useful port."

In all, more than a million soldiers trained in central Louisiana between 1939 and 1945, infusing millions of dollars into the Louisiana economy. By October 1940, about 8,000 workmen were employed in construction jobs at Camps Beauregard and Livingston. By January 1941, 36,887 civilians were working in one capacity or another at the camps. Local suppliers to these camps provided a wide variety of goods, including about $12,000 per day worth of gasoline for Army vehicles and, a reminder of the times, $600 a day in stove wood, according to Sanson.

Over the longer term, the maneuvers helped introduce or reintroduce Louisiana to military leaders who located other installations such as England Air Force Base in Alexandria, Chennault Air Force Base at Lake Charles, and the Naval Air Station at New Iberia, all of which have now been closed, and enlarged facilities such as Barksdale Air Force Base in Shreveport, best known in recent times as the "secure place" where President George W. Bush first stopped during the early uncertainties of the terror attacks on September 11, 2001.

Louisiana was selected in 1940 for maneuvers by Gen. Stanley D. Embick of the U.S. Army Fourth Corps Area, which was headquartered in Atlanta. The first maneuvers began in May 1940 and eventually involved more than 70,000 troops spread over Rapides,

Natchitoches, Sabine, and Vernon Parishes. There would be more maneuvers in 1941, 1942, and 1943.

The Army liked the area and — although there were some abuses of privileges — the area liked the Army, or at least the Army's pay. In May 1940, for example, the Alexandria Town Talk reported, "Every roadside establishment in the local area was crowded with troopers … and while they were here, there was a steady tinkle of cash drawers in every establishment where refreshments and sandwiches could be obtained."

According to Sanson, the 1940 maneuvers alone cost $87,000 per day in soldier pay and goods and services purchased, and a good bit of it stayed in Louisiana. And, he says, "the 1941 Louisiana Maneuvers easily eclipsed the magnitude of the 1940 exercises."

Aside from being what Sanson calls "a landmark in the development of the U.S. Army's strategy and planning for war," the military activities also provided a huge impetus to the local economy.

"The Army payroll for the last part of August [1941], was the largest in Shreveport up to that date," he reports, "approximately $900,000 issued through the Commercial National Bank. Alexandria merchants stocked their shelves in anticipation of extra-heavy business, and they were not disappointed. Most of them remained open on Labor Day, and troops crowded stores in the maneuver area, sometimes buying out a store's entire stock, especially tobacco, candy, and refreshments. Theaters and restaurants both experienced continuous lines for seats, and some smaller store owners reported selling as much in a day as they normally sold in a year. One study of the maneuvers estimate that they were worth about $25 million to the state."

The fledgling flying field that became Barksdale Air Force Base may have been the reason that Patton was given the war games orders to capture Shreveport in 1941, and he did it in the same, unorthodox way that would bring him notoriety in World War II. He took his division on a 380-mile encircling maneuver deep into Texas and then came at Shreveport from the rear, through marshy land near Caddo Lake that had been presumed

*82nd Infantry Division standing "Retreat" following Sgt. Alvin C. York's address to the division, Camp Claiborne, May 7, 1942. The first assembly of the division since reactivation.*
Courtesy Newcomb Camera and Art Supply, Mary Pearce Hart collection

*Gypsy Rose Lee at Camp Livingston in the 1940s.*

*Below: Brewster Company munitions plant, Shreveport, 1944.*

impregnable to tanks.

These maneuvers made Patton's command reputation and stalled the careers of other officers. Generals who did not perform well in the war games were weeded out and, when the real shooting war started, were left behind in charge of training or other stateside duties. Another soldier who came into his own during the games was Col. Dwight D. Eisenhower, who was 3rd Army Chief of Staff.

During the early years of the war in Europe, before Pearl Harbor, most Louisianians watched the headlines with concern, but agreed with many other Americans who felt strongly that there was no place for Americans in the latest European conflict. They remembered the worry and loss when GIs crossed the Atlantic to fight during World War I. This time, many argued, we should let the Europeans settle the fight among themselves.

In those early years, local newspapers reported the war news, but displayed just as prominently events of only local significance. Celebrations such as the Mardi Gras pageantry in Lafayette continued through 1941 before "going dark" for the rest of the war.

As the United States edged toward war, the headlines began to suggest a change in attitude. Plans were announced in Baton Rouge to begin training Louisiana youths for defense jobs, parishes began setting up local "defense committees" and organizing teams of aircraft observers to watch for potential enemy planes, World War I veterans were asked to register

for "national defense service," and fishermen who worked the Gulf of Mexico from Louisiana were asked to bring their skills to the Merchant Marine Naval Reserve.

After Americans entered the war, Louisianians joined with the nation in grumbling about rationing of everything from tires to sugar, knitting sweaters and socks for "our boys" overseas, planting Victory Gardens, and scrounging for scrap metal to be turned into tanks and bullets. A "Cajun Coast Guard" was formed in lower Louisiana to watch for German submarines, which took a frightful toll on tankers moving oil and refined petroleum products to and from Louisiana refineries. Unlikely organizations such as the "Victory Pig Club" sprang up, in which farmers were encouraged to raise a pig, sell it, and use the profits to buy war bonds.

And, across Louisiana, mothers hung Gold Stars in their windows for loved ones who would never return. According to a War Department report issued in 1946, there were 3,964 World War II casualties from Louisiana. As expected, Orleans Parish ranked first on that sorrowful list with 773. Others in the top ten were Caddo (320), East Baton Rouge (150), Rapides (146), Calcasieu (135), Ouachita (114), Jefferson (89), Acadia (86), Vermilion (82), and Lafayette and St. Landry (81 each).

Returning veterans found that the end of the war did not mean the end of wartime economies. Thousands of newlyweds found that there were not enough homes. Rationing

*Members of the Coast Guard Patrol, formed shortly after the start of World War II to guard Southwest Pass, Freshwater Bayou, and Grand Isle, 1940s.*
Courtesy Louis J. Perret, Clerk of Court, Lafayette Parish

*B-29 bomber over Barksdale Air Force Base, 1940s.*
U. S. Army Corps photo courtesy Noel Memorial Library Archives, LSU in Shreveport PC1046

continued until the economy was able to adjust itself again from an effort devoted almost entirely to the war machine to one providing for the peacetime.

Boys who had been recruited from the farms of rural Louisiana came home and stayed in the cities. Every urban area — New Orleans, Baton Rouge, Shreveport, Alexandria, Monroe, Lake Charles, Lafayette — saw the beginnings of a continuing trend of quickly rising populations.

New consumer goods came to Louisiana as they did to the rest of the nation, so that by 1950 more than half of the people of the state had traded in their horse-drawn transportation for a car or pickup truck. As the Rural Electrification Administration began to spread lines through the state, even remote farm homes acquired electric lights, then washing machines and refrigerators.

Television sets and a bigger part of the American Dream were not far behind for most of Louisiana — for most of its citizens. That dream was still far, far away for most of the black people of the state.

As historian Bennett H. Wall points out in his history of the state, "The historic division of [Louisiana] society into white and black had by 1950 hardened into a permanent caste system. Although a few blacks could vote, oppressive racial laws subjected them to political, social, and economic discrimination. … The expectation of economic freedom raised by the New Deal and visions of brotherhood raised by World War II did not include blacks."

**Below and opposite page:** *World War II parade down 3rd Street, Alexandria, circa 1941.*
Courtesy Newcomb Camera and Art Supply, Joe Dellmon Collection at Cammie G. Henry Research Center, Eugene P. Watson Memorial Library, Northwestern State University

*Louisiana Purchase: A Pictorial Retrospective Celebrating Louisiana*

**Above:** *Texas & Pacific Railway train No. 20 from Marshall, Texas, to Alexandria. Photo taken from the Anna Street viaduct, Shreveport, 1943. Walter Simpson was the engineer.* Courtesy Noel Memorial Library Archives, LSU in Shreveport PC1162

**Opposite page:** *Texax & Pacific Railway "The Bullet." Photo taken from the Anna Street viaduct, Shreveport, 1942.*
Courtesy Noel Memorial Library Archives, LSU in Shreveport PC1160: Ed Robinson, photographer

**Above:** *Cotton compress between Grolee and Bellevue streets, Opelousas, 1940s. It was destroyed by fire in 1954.*
Courtesy Opelousas Museum and Interpretive Center

**Right:** *Jimmie H. Davis "the singing governor" visiting Shreveport mayor Clyde Fant in the 1940s. Davis managed careers both in Louisiana politics (serving first as Shreveport's commissioner of public safety and later two terms as governor), as well as a performing career that included more than 50 albums, ten movies, and induction into the Country Music Hall of Fame.*
Courtesy Noel Memorial Library Archives, LSU in Shreveport 1537B: Jack Barham Collection

**Below:** *Downtown Alexandria, 1940s. Old City Hall on the right.*
Courtesy Newcomb Camera and Art Supply, Delores Guillory Dekko Collection

**Above:** *Louisiana native Huddie Ledbetter, a.k.a. Leadbelly, performs in the 1940s. Ledbetter was born on the Jeter Plantation near Mooringsport in 1885.*

Courtesy Noel Memorial Library Archives, LSU in Shreveport PD128

**Right:** *Carding cotton in Lafayette, 1945.*

Courtesy Louis J. Perret, Clerk of Court, Lafayette Parish

**Left:** *Camp Claiborne telephone exchange, November, 1945.*
Courtesy Newcomb Camera and Art Supply, Edward Flynn Collection

**Below:** *Third Street, looking southeast, Alexandria, 1946.*
Courtesy Newcomb Camera and Art Supply, Central Louisiana Electric Collection

**Above:** *Knights of Columbus installation parade, Opelousas, 1946.*
Courtesy Opelousas Museum and Interpretive Center

**Right:** *Louisiana Yambilee Parade, Opelousas, 1946.*
Courtesy Opelousas Museum and Interpretive Center

**Below:** *Rodeo parade on Third Street, Alexandria, August 23, 1949.*
Courtesy Newcomb Camera and Art Supply, A.C. Irby Collection

**Above:** *Anne Anderson Hedgecock Terzia, left, and Scootie Day Huff ride a float during a parade in Shreveport, 1949.* Courtesy Noel Memorial Library Archives, LSU in Shreveport PC578: Graham's Studio photo

**Right:** *Holiday in Dixie court, Shreveport, 1949. Left to right: Ellen Clarke, Alice Murray Stacy, Norma Ann McCook Hendrick Hardy, Gloria Chastain Flowers, Anne Anderson Hedgecock, Julia Norfleet Hearne, Renee Calder, Gloria Clauson Davis, Mary Beth Fiser Schober, and Scootie Day Huff.*
Courtesy Noel Memorial Library Archives, LSU in Shreveport PC642: Graham's Studio photo

**Below:** *Crowds from throughout south Louisiana attend the opening of the Evangeline Maid Bread baking plant on Sunrise and St. John streets in Lafayette, 1949.*
Courtesy Louis J. Perret, Clerk of Court, Lafayette Parish

## CHAPTER NINE

1950 - 1999

# Changing Times

*O*n *July 1, 1952,* the Highway Revenue Act of 1952 went into effect, authorizing construction of 2,500 miles of Interstate highway across the United States. The system of highways that would be created changed the face of Louisiana just as the coming of the railways had undone the age of the steamboat.

As modern highways began to cross the state, trucks that delivered goods to the doorstep began to carry more and more of the cargo once carried in rail cars, once again changing the physical face of Louisiana. Towns on the interstate system grew and prospered, those that were bypassed did not.

But it was a political change, not a physical one that most occupied the minds of the people of Louisiana.

The issue, the politicians said, was "state's rights." The fight was over school desegregation. Louisiana did not go through riots as some other places did over this and other civil rights issues during the 1950s and especially the turbulent 1960s, but there was plenty of rancor.

In May 1954, the U.S. Supreme Court decided the landmark case of *Brown v. the Board of Education of Topeka,* outlawing racial segregation in the schools. This directly affected the way Louisiana education "worked," and threatened a whole way of life. The issues quickly became much broader than that of who would sit in what classroom.

The Supreme Court ruling brought to a head a whole range of issues arising not only out of "separate but equal" schools, but also public accommodations and public attitudes that had kept the races at arm's length since the Civil War. White Louisiana felt threatened, and scared — and reacted with White Citizens' Councils and similar organizations all too reminiscent of those formed during the Reconstruction era.

Black people, with the aid of new federal legislation, responded by registering to vote in record numbers and becoming much more active in the political arena, and, in the process, changing long-standing political equations. A coalition of south Louisiana whites and black people from across the state elected Edwin Edwards in 1974, the first governor from south Louisiana since the reform election of 1940 — and, some say, reestablished a

*Opposite Page: Elvis Presley's first national Louisiana Hayride appearance, in Shreveport with Scotty Moore on guitar, and Bill Black on bass, October 16, 1954.*

Courtesy Noel Memorial Library Archives, LSU in Shreveport: Langston McEachern, photographer

*St. Landry Parish Training School students, 1950.*
Courtesy Opelousas Museum and Interpretive Center

new era of chicanery that had not been seen since that reform election. In 1977, a similar coalition elected Ernest N. (Dutch) Morial as the first black mayor of New Orleans.

But despite the turmoil of the 1950s and 1960s, Louisiana began to develop its industrial base more than it had ever done before — particularly in the petrochemical corridor that stretches along the Mississippi River between New Orleans and Baton Rouge and, to a lesser degree, along the Calcasieu River in southwest Louisiana. Huge plants began to turn out gasoline, diesel fuel, petroleum distillates, paint, fertilizers, insecticides, and other petroleum derivatives.

*Sit-in at Walgreen's, Shreveport, July 1963.*
Courtesy Noel Memorial Library Archives, LSU in Shreveport:
Jack Barnam, photographer

In coastal Louisiana, the offshore oil industry began to blossom, as huge production rigs were built at inland ports and towed into the Gulf of Mexico. Urban areas grew as agribusiness began to substitute for the family farm, and rural families moved to town. One of the state's worst tragedies rolled ashore from the Gulf on June 27, 1957, when Hurricane Audrey pushed a tidal wave through coastal southwest Louisiana, claiming more than 500 lives and leaving behind millions upon millions of dollars in debris.

Industrial growth and the population increase that came with it spurred growth in other sectors of the economy, particularly in the urban service, retail, and trade centers. That growth, in turn, set off still more change as so-called "big box" retailers, food franchisers, and mall builders began to move into Louisiana's urban areas — in many instances replacing long-standing local businesses and changing the face and character of the communities.

The Census Bureau now recognizes eight Metropolitan Statistical Areas in Louisiana, each of them an urban center that has an expanded role and population as the government, service, medical, and trade center for a large region of the state.

But even as the modern, auto-, television-, Web site-, franchise-, absentee-owner-driven growth continues to remake the face and character of Louisiana, its unique cultures survive, colorful pasts woven into the unique tapestry that is Louisiana.

*Shreveport and parish officers use tear gas to break up a protest near Booker T. Washington High School, September 23, 1963.*
Courtesy Noel Memorial Library Archives, LSU in Shreveport: Lloyd Stilley, photographer

*St. James senior class, Alexandria, 1955.*
Courtesy Newcomb Camera and Art Supply

**Above:** *Crowd at Lafayette Southern Pacific Depot waiting for arrival of Dudley LeBlanc with Hadacol Caravan and movie stars in the 1950s. The Brown News building can be seen in the background.*

Courtesy Louis J. Perret, Clerk of Court, Lafayette Parish

**Right:** *Actor/singer Jimmy Durante with Dudley LeBlanc during Hadacol Days, Lafayette, 1950s.*

Courtesy Louis J. Perret, Clerk of Court, Lafayette Parish

**Below:** *Hadacol Extravaganza at Blackham Coliseum, Lafayette, 1950.*

Courtesy Louis J. Perret, Clerk of Court, Lafayette Parish

Left: *Fourth and Murray, Alexandria, 1955.* Courtesy Newcomb Camera and Art Supply

Below: *Aerial view looking toward Endom Traffic Bridge, which connects West Monroe to Monroe, 1951.* Courtesy Ouachita Parish Public Library, Special Archives Collection

**Right:** *Mike Fisher of the Alexandria Police Department on the department's first motorcycle, 1950s.*
Courtesy Newcomb Camera and Art Supply, Mike Fisher Collection

**Right:** *First Communion, St. James Catholic Church, Alexandria, April 19, 1953.* Courtesy Newcomb Camera and Art Supply

**Below:** *First Annual Dog Show in Arbalado Subdivision on Clark Court Street off of Johnston next to UL in Lafayette. The show was organized by Charles de Gravelles. Among those pictured are Bobby Theriot, Leah Lane, J.J. Burdin, Ann de Gravelles, Lenny Lou Martin, Carroll Pooler, Ben Pooler, Jean Delaney, Cheramie Hebert, Joanie Morvant, Leslie Seale, Midge Bates and Linda Lane.*
Courtesy Louis J. Perret, Clerk of Court, Lafayette Parish

Left: *Motorcycles lined up in front of Howard Griffin motor shop on South Grand Street, Monroe, in the 1950s. In later years, Howard Griffin grew into a large boat and motor business and a large toy store, "Howard Griffin's Land of Toys."*
Courtesy News-Star archives

Right: *Fourth grade class of Millsaps Elementary School, West Monroe, 1955.*

Courtesy News-Star archives

Below:: *Alexandria Aces baseball team, 1956.*
Courtesy Newcomb Camera and
Art Supply, Sherman Miller Collection

**Above:** *Zydeco legend Clifton Chenier performing in Opelousas, circa 1965.*
Courtesy Opelousas Museum and Interpretive Center

**Above:** *Minus Breaux operates a cotton picker on the Antoine Boudreaux Farm, Lafayette Parish in 1962.*
Courtesy Louis J. Perret, Clerk of Court, Lafayette Parish

**Right:** *Making "Boucherie." Shown here preparing the hog are, left to right: Inez B. Trahan, Antoine Bou-dreaux, Etienne Vallot and John Credeur. Opta Trahan is kneeling behind Inez. Photo was taken in April 1961 at the home of Mr. and Mrs. Antoine Boudreaux.*
Courtesy Louis J. Perret, Clerk of Court, Lafayette Parish

**Below:** *Squad of advanced infantry trainees are ac-quainted with topography duplicating that of the deserts of North Africa for training purposes at Fort Polk, May 1970.* U. S. Army photo courtesy Noel Memorial Library Archives, LSU in Shreveport

**Above:** *Shreveport Mayor Clyde Fant with Sports Award Winners, 1970. Terry Bradshaw is holding the trophy.*
Courtesy Noel Memorial Library Archives,
LSU in Shreveport PC1879: Ben Kinel, photographer

**Right:** *Natchitoches Christmas Festival, December 7, 1980.*
Courtesy Noel Memorial Library Archives,
LSU in Shreveport T78222

**Below:** *Construction of the First Federal Plaza in downtown Shreveport, 1981. The building was later sold to the city and became Shreveport's new city hall in 2000.* Courtesy The Times archives

**Above:** *Natchitoches Folk Festival, July 21, 1985.*
Courtesy Noel Memorial Library Archives, LSU in Shreveport 92646

Above: *In March 1980, Monroe Regional Airport was "Reagan Country." Ronald Reagan, presidential hopeful, made a quick stop at the airport for a brief but enthusiastic rally by area supporters. He was elected president that year. As president in January 1993, Reagan returned to the city to offer hope and comfort during a flood.*
Courtesy The News-Star archives

Above: *Willis Prudhomme, 1980s.*
Courtesy Opelousas Museum and Interpretive Center

Above: *The finishing touches were put on Pecanland Mall in Monroe in May 1985. The new mall attracted attention from throughout northeastern Louisiana. It was a boon to the area economy, with 910,000 square feet of shopping area.* Courtesy The News-Star archives

Right: *In 1986 Cuban prisoners at the Oakdale Immigration Detention Center rioted and set a large part of the prison on fire after taking guards hostages. The five-day standoff focused the eyes of the nation and the world on Central Louisiana. The siege ended peacefully and no fatalities were reported.* Courtesy The News-Star archives

**Above:** *In the 1980's and 1990's Interstate 49 connecting I-20 in Shreveport to I-10 in Lafayette was designed and built. The Interstate provided a much-needed link from north to south Louisiana.*

**Above:** *St. Vincent's Academy. The 119-year-old private school closed in 1988 due to declining enrollments.* Courtesy The Times archives

**Right:** *Relatives and friends of soldiers returning to Louisiana from Desert Storm wait for transport airplanes to arrive at England Air Force Base in 1991. Shortly after this the base was closed as an Air Force military installation.*

**Below:** *Past Mardi Gras queens, Lafayette, 1992.* Courtesy Louis J. Perret, Clerk of Court, Lafayette Parish

## CHAPTER TEN

# Today's Louisiana

*Two hundred years have passed* since the United States flag was first raised over New Orleans. Throughout the past two centuries no other state in the Union has had a more varied or colorful history than Louisiana. We have had a past of many battles, on the battlefield and in the political arena. Our architecture is a lasting impression of French and Spanish rule. Our museums, plantations, historic sites and attractions serve as reminders of a unique and intriguing past that helped shape both our state and the nation.

Louisiana has been blessed with a unique array of cultures not found in any other state or nation. These diverse cultures melded together have resulted in food, music and a way of life unlike anywhere else. The unique Zydeco music...the birthplace of jazz... the bountiful pot of crawfish on the boiler... the tantalizing gumbo simmering in the pot. And where else can you find Mardi Gras celebrated all over the state?

Although modern communications and the general diffusion of cultural differences are helping to blur some of the distinctions, today's Louisiana is comprised of five regions, each with their own unique culture and customs; Cajun Country (south), Plantation Country (east), the Crossroads (central), Sportsman's Paradise (north) and Greater New Orleans.

Much of the western part of the state has been more closely allied with Texas and its cowboys than with other parts of Louisiana. Shreveport resembles Dallas much more than it does New Orleans. The rolling hills and pine forests of the northern part of the state are far removed in distance and geology from the swamps, marshes, and *prairies tremblantes* – waterlogged "trembling prairies" – of the southern parishes.

Each region offers distinct cultural nuances, but the common generalization that north Louisiana is "American" and south Louisiana is "French" is true only as far as generalizations can be trusted. There are many cultural influences in all of the state, including French, Spanish, American, Acadian, African, German, Italian, Irish, Caribbean, and others from practically every part of the globe – it is a matter of degree and emphasis. Our cultures complement one another, which makes Louisiana one-of-a-kind.

Louisiana's exciting attractions are as diverse as our many cultures. From the casinos and nightlife, to plantations and museums, to restaurants, music venues and marinas, there is a lot to experience in Louisiana. We take great pride in what our state has to offer and enjoy sharing our culture with friends and neighbors all over the world.

In the spring of 1999, the Louisiana Economic Development Council issued a report

Opposite page:
*Alexandria Zoo visitors smile in awe at the holiday cheer.*
Courtesy The Town Talk archives

called "Louisiana: Vision 2020," that attempted to look twenty years into the new century and predict the state of the state. The optimistic report sets high goals for the first two decades of the twenty-first century: "Louisiana will have a vibrant, balanced economy; a fully engaged, well-educated workforce; and a quality of life that places it among the top ten states in which to live, work, visit, and do business."

The council set three primary goals for positioning our state for growth and expansion.

**Goal 1:** Re-create Louisiana as a learning enterprise in which all Louisiana businesses, institutions, and citizens are actively involved in the pursuit of knowledge, and where that knowledge is deployed to improve the competitiveness of business, the efficiency of governmental institutions, and the quality of life of citizens.

**Goal 2:** Create an economy driven by diverse and thriving technology-intensive industries that actively utilize Louisiana's colleges and universities as a source of well-educated graduates as employees, a source of expertise for problem solving, and a source of technology of commercialization.

**Goal 3:** To have a standard of living ranked among the top ten states in America, and safe, healthy communities where rich natural and cultural assets continue to make Louisiana a unique place to live, work, and do business.

*Below: Horse and carriage ride on Dumaine Street, French Quarter, New Orleans.*
Courtesy Louisiana Office of Tourism

"Louisiana: Vision 2020" is an aggressive plan and while our state has many challenges ahead in order to achieve these goals, improvements have been made and noted nationally. Many of the positive things about our state and the improvements Louisiana is making can be viewed on the Internet at http://www.lded.state.la.us/overview/la_positives.asp.

**Above:** *Night view of downtown Shreveport.*
Courtesy The Times archives

# Louisiana "Positives"

As we celebrate the Bicentennial of the Louisiana Purchase, we celebrate our accomplishments, while continuing to strive for a better Louisiana today, tomorrow and always.

- Louisiana is first in dollars spent for historic preservation. Louisiana spent more than a third of a billion in fiscal year 2000, creating more than 9,000 jobs (National Park Service).

- Louisiana was second in tourism growth in 2000. The state saw 2.2 million more visitors in 2000 than in 1999, for an increase of 22 percent (Travel Industry Association of America).

- Louisiana is the most improved state in the United Way State of Caring Index, which measures the social and economic health of the nation. The index covers areas such as health, education, civic engagement, safety and other quality-of-life areas. Chief area of improvement was public school per pupil expenditure. Louisiana increased K-12 funding to three times the national level (from 1988 to 1998). And Louisiana's support to non-profit groups grew more than 70 percent, almost double the national rate.

- The Forbes/Milken Institute placed all seven of Louisiana's metropolitan areas on its list of best places for business and careers (Forbes Magazine, May 2002).

- Two Louisiana cities were ranked among the nation's top wealth builders according to the Brookings Institution Center on Urban and Metropolitan Policy based on areas that despite population growth below the median, had real per-capita income growth above the median (Feb. 2002).

- Louisiana is among the most

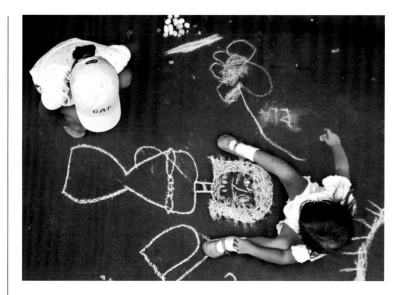

**Above:** *Seven-year-old Elaine Simon, left, colors on the sidewalk outside Forsythe Tennis Courts with friend, three-year-old Hannah Taylor.*

Courtesy The News-Star archives

improved states in the Milken Institute's New Economy Index, which ranks each state, based upon 12 criteria that Milken Institute research has determined are critical to a region's future high-tech growth. (Milken Institute, Nov. 2001).

- Louisiana's LA 4 early childhood education program has been highlighted by the National Association of State Boards of Education as a model initiative (NASBE, Sept. 2002).

- The Center for Public Integrity ranked Louisiana 15th for its political parties financial disclosure system. Openness, accountability and public access were the primary focus of the nationwide study (The Center for Public Integrity, Oct. 2002).

- According to the United States Bureau of Economic Analysis, Louisiana's workforce is the fourth-most productive in the country and 1st in fewest hours lost due to work-related accidents.

- Louisiana leads the nation in the percentage of African-American visitors last year with 13.4 percent (Travel Industry Association of America, September 2002).

• The Center for Digital Government ranked Louisiana 2nd in Digital Democracy, based on access to laws, candidate information and electronic voting technologies, in its 2002 Digital State Survey.

• Louisiana climbed from 25th to 17th for e-commerce and Business Regulation, which evaluates the availability of business information, the ability to conduct business online, and the status of portals and e-procurement systems (The Center for Digital Government, Aug. 2002).

• Louisiana climbed to No. 18 in the Small Business Survival Index, which rates the policy climate for small business in each state by calculating government costs to business (Small Business Survival Committee, July 2002).

• Louisiana's START program is in the Top 5 in 529 investment plans in the country, after netting 6.33 percent interest last year (Saving for College, July 2002).

**Above:** *Bell tower at Louisiana State University, Baton Rouge.*
Courtesy Louisiana Office of Tourism

• Seven Louisiana businesses made the BE 100 – which annually ranks the nation's largest black-owned businesses (Black Enterprise Magazine, July 2002).

• Louisiana ranked 19th in the country in terms of high-tech job growth for 2001. The state's three-percent growth was higher than the national growth rate of just one percent (American Electronics Association, July 2002).

• Three out of the four 2001 SAFE award winners were companies whose offshore divisions are run out of Louisiana. The best in the oil and natural gas industry are annually recognized for safe operations, environmental stewardship and fiscal responsibility (Minerals Management Services, July 2002).

• Louisiana ranked in the Top 10 in the nation (7th) in The Princeton Review's first Annual Ranking of State Accountability Systems. The ranking is based on the state's complete accountability system, including academic alignment, test quality, openness to public scrutiny and education policy goals of the state (The Princeton Review, June 2002).

• Louisiana ranked 5th in the percentage of manufacturing establishments with Internet Access in the Progressive Policy Institute's 2002 New Economy Index (Public Policy Institute, June 2002).

• Louisiana remains in the top 10 in the prestigious Bloomberg annual tax survey, which cites assessment differences from state to state and then ranks them for their tax friendliness. "A" for tax friendliness to retirees (4th nationally), "B+" for tax friendliness to families (9th nationally). (Bloomberg Personal Finance, May 2002).

• Louisiana is ranked 4th-best state for e-commerce based on how state laws, regulations, and administrative actions support Internet use by Louisiana citizens (Progressive Policy Institute, March 2002).

• Louisiana has been recognized as one of the Top 10 states in the nation in overall education reform, 4th in the nation in standards and accountability, and 16th in improving teacher quality (Education Week, January 2002).

• Louisiana is ranked 3rd in the nation in the percentage of accessibility to public and private institutions (Lumina Foundation, January 2002).

- Louisiana has climbed to 2nd in the nation in percentage increase over the last year in funding for postsecondary education. Over the last five years, Louisiana has attained a ranking of fourth in the nation in percentage increase in postsecondary funding (Grapevine Center for Higher Education and Educational Finance, January 2002).

- The Louisiana Youth ChalleNGe Program, a 17-month program targeting high school dropouts, has been selected as the top ChalleNGe program for Responsible Citizen and Leadership/Followership (National Guard Bureau, February 2002).

- The Louisiana Department of Public Safety and Corrections has been recognized by the Commission on Accreditation for Corrections as one of only three in the country that has achieved full accreditation of its system. (ACA, November 2001).

- Louisiana's Department of Social Services was one of only 11 states in the country to receive enhanced funding from USDA, Food and Nutrition Services for fiscal year 2000. This was based on the state's Food Stamp payment error rate of 5.66% – the national average was 8.91%. This low error rate is especially notable since Louisiana ranks 10th in the nation in the amount of food stamp benefits issued (Center on Budget & Policy Priorities, April 2001).

- The most recent study undertaken by the Department of Health and Hospitals Office for Addictive Disorders shows that Louisiana continues to meet the goal of keeping illegal rate of retail tobacco sales below its goal of 10 percent, with a rate of 8.5 percent, one of the lowest rates in

**Above:** *Little girl offers a peach to her friend at the Ruston Peach Festival.*
Courtesy Louisiana Office of Tourism

**Below:** *Sunset at Caddo Lake Cypress Point.*
Courtesy The Times archives

**Above:** *Dancers in Festival International parade, Lafayette.*
Courtesy Louisiana Office of Tourism

**Below:** *Musicians beat drums in the Festival International parade.*
Courtesy Louisiana Office of Tourism

the nation (DHH/Office of Addictive Disorders, November 2001).

• Louisiana is ranked 45th in per capita taxation (U.S. Census Bureau, 2001).

• Louisiana has maintained its B- grade over the past three years in the Maxwell School of Citizenship & Public Affairs annual ranking of state government performance (Maxwell School, 2001).

• Louisiana is in the top 10 in Most New and Expanded Corporate Facilities (9th nationally) and Capital Investment per million residents (3rd) (Site Selection magazine, March 2001).

• Louisiana ranked in the top 20 (19th) for small-business friendly states (Small business Survival Index, 2001).

• Louisiana jumped from its traditional rankings of 1st or 2nd in the EPA's Toxics Release Inventory to 12th in 1999 (last available report) while increasing productivity. The annual survey ranks states based on their amount of toxic chemical releases and other waste management activities reported by manufacturing facilities. The vast majority of these gains were accomplished through Louisiana's industry-based voluntary Responsible Care Program.

• Louisiana is 8th in the nation for new manufacturing plants with 68 (Site Selection magazine, 2000).

• Louisiana's ranking for its use of technology in government has climbed from 44th to 18th (Center for Digital Government, 2000).

*Source: Louisiana Economic Development "Louisiana Positives" page on the Internet at http://www.lded.state.la.us/overview/la_positives.asp*

Above: *Bayou at Acadian Village, Lafayette.* Courtesy Louisiana Office of Tourism

Below: *A rose in one of the many rose gardens surrounding the Carillon Tower at the American Rose Center, Greenwood. The American Rose Center features North America's largest rose garden with more than 20,000 roses on 118 acres of blooming beauty. The center is headquarters for the American Rose Society.* Courtesy The Times archives

Above: *Tickfaw blacksmith Jim Jenkins makes a plant hanger at the Louisiana Folklife Festival in Monroe.*
Courtesy The News-Star archives

Below: *Melissa Cooke of Houston takes some Easter day photographs of her children, MacKenzie Cooke and Zac Cooke, at the Norton Art Gallery's azalea gardens, Shreveport.*
Courtesy The Times archives

Above: *St. Joseph's Catholic Church, Baton Rouge.*
Courtesy Louisiana Office of Tourism

**Right:** *Natchitoches historic district from across the Cane River Lake.*
Courtesy Louisiana Office of Tourism

**Below:** *Historic Front Street in Natchitoches is a scenic backdrop for Louisiana foilage.*
Courtesy The Town Talk archives

**Above:** *Sunflowers in full bloom at Gordon Boogaert's field located on Hwy 3049 just north of Shreveport. Boogaert's field is part of the Annual Sunflower Trail.* Courtesy The Times archives

**Below:** *Thousands of Christmas lights illuminate Natchitoches and the Cane River.* Courtesy Louisiana Office of Tourism

Left: *Red River Revel at night in the Festival Plaza in downtown Shreveport. Home to the Red River Revel, as well as MudBug Madness, Holiday in Dixie, Let the Good Times Roll and dozens of other annual festivals, Shreveport's Festival Plaza hosts millions of visitors each year.* Courtesy The Times archives

Above: *Vaughn Womack stirs some boiling crawfish during the 2002 MudBug Madness festival. Shaver's Catering had both of these pots cooking 120lbs each.* Courtesy The Times archives

Below: *The streets of downtown Winnsboro are filled for the 16th Annual Franklin Parish Catfish Festival.* Courtesy The News-Star archives

Above: *The French Quarter Festival winds its way through the Quarter, New Orleans.* Courtesy Louisiana Office of Tourism

Above: *Chelsea Crenshaw runs from the splashing water as she plays near the fountain at Riverfront Park, Shreveport.* Courtesy The Times archives

Left: *People gather to listen to jazz clarinetist in the French Quarter, New Orleans.*
Courtesy Louisiana Office of Tourism

Below: *Shreveport Regional Art Council's "Once in a Millennium Moon" by Meg Saligman, dedicated in January 2001. Local residents and community leaders assisted in painting the record-breaking public mural – the largest in the nation.*
Courtesy The Times archives

**Above:** *Fog blankets the Red River as the early morning sun lights downtown Shreveport.*
Courtesy The Times archives

**Left:** *Fountain in the courtyard of a French Quarter hotel, New Orleans.*
Courtesy Louisiana Office of Tourism

**Below:** *The Melrose Art Festival at the Melrose Plantation in Natchitoches is always a crowd favorite.* Courtesy The Town Talk archives

Above: *Riders begin Courir de Mardi Gras in Elton.* Courtesy Louisiana Office of Tourism

Above: *Cindy Dickson throws a soccer ball into the screaming crowd during the Krewe of Gemini Mardi Gras Parade in Shreveport.* Courtesy The Times archives

Left: *Mardi Gras float in Rex Parade on Canal Street, New Orleans.* Courtesy Louisiana Office of Tourism

Below: *Spanish Town Mardis Gras parade on Spanish Town Road in Baton Rouge.* Courtesy Louisiana Office of Tourism

**Above:** *Hands reach out for trinkets and beads at the Mardi Gras parade in downtown Lafayette.* Courtesy Louisiana Office of Tourism

**Above, left:** *The Louisiana tradition of Mardi Gras is alive and well with these Alexandria youngsters.* Courtesy The Town Talk archives

**Below:** *King Janus rules over Mardi Gras parade in downtown Monroe.*
Courtesy Louisiana Office of Tourism

**Above:** *Aqua tunnel at the Aquarium of the Americas and IMAX Theatre in New Orleans.*
Courtesy Louisiana Office of Tourism

**Right:** *Shatarica Hill has had her fill of food and fun and sleeps in her stroller as her father Tariq pushes her along at the Let the Good Times Roll festival in Shreveport.* Courtesy The Times archives

**Below:** *Sunset at Alligator Bayou, Baton Rouge.* Courtesy Louisiana Office of Tourism

**Above:** *One of today's most recognizable landmarks for the Shreveport-Bossier area, the "Neon Bridge" links the two cities across the Red River near downtown, and is seen here as a backdrop for the area's fireworks exhibits. Commissioned by the Shreveport Regional Art Council in 1993, the "Neon Bridge" public art was sculpted by nationally respected light sculptor Rockne Krebs. The "Neon Bridge" consists of 7,000 feet of neon making it the nation's largest neon sculpture.* Courtesy The Times archives

**Below:** *Daniel Castillo waits with friends for the Grand Entry of the "Tunica-Biloxi Powwow" in Marksville.* Courtesy The Town Talk archives

**Above:** *Lobby of historic Bentley Hotel in Alexandria.* Courtesy Louisiana Office of Tourism

**Left:** *Strawberries displayed by festival participant at the Strawberry Festival in Pontchatoula.*
Courtesy Louisiana Office of Tourism

**Right:** *Paddling a canoe on Alligator Bayou, Manchac area.*
Courtesy Louisiana Office of Tourism

**Right:** *Union troops firing at battle of Port Hudson reenactment, Port Hudson State Historic Site.*
Courtesy Louisiana Office of Tourism

**Below:** *Students at Byrd High School received national attention when they created giant flags in the front windows of the school to showcase their patriotism and solidarity following the September 11, 2001 terrorist attacks.*
Courtesy The Times archives

**Above:** *Fathers dressed in plaid mini-skirts, sandals, wigs and tank tops and some shaved their face, stomach and arms per their children's request. The dads were battling for tickets for the upcoming Britney Spears concert at CenturyTel Center in Shreveport.* Courtesy The Town Talk archives

**Below:** *The regal Delta Queen makes its way up the Red River.* Courtesy The Town Talk archives

**Above:** *Rachel Luneau spins in the night breeze as a princess while celebrating Halloween at Calvary Baptist Church in Alexandria.* Courtesy The Town Talk archives

**Left:** *A duck hunter crouches in the marsh and calls for unsuspecting prey.*
Courtesy The Town Talk archives

**Above:** *Louisiana egrets welcome an unexpected visitor.* Courtesy The Town Talk archives

**Below:** *The Super Derby at Louisiana Downs in Bossier City.* Courtesy The Times archives

**Above:** *Sailing and sailboarding on Lake Charles.* Courtesy Louisiana Office of Tourism

**Below:** *Houmas House Plantation, Darrow.* Courtesy Louisiana Office of Tourism

**Above:** *Sixteen year-old Jonathan Gibson of Monroe prepares to hit his ball at the Chennault Park Driving Range.* Courtesy The News-Star archives

**Left:** *Nell Walters, right, throws a large snowball at grand daughter Beth Gordon during a rare snowfall in Monroe.* Courtesy The News-Star archives

**Above:** *Wal-Mart Bass Fishing League participants Jesse Hoover of Oakland, California (left) and Danny Hall of Ellijay, Georgia (standing) try their luck under the I-220 Cross Lake Bridge.* Courtesy The Times archives

**Below:** *The Kent House dance troupe rehearses a square dance rendition.*
Courtesy The Town Talk archives

**Above:** *Musician plays the washboard at Zydeco Music Festival in Plaisance.* Courtesy Louisiana Office of Tourism

**Below:** *Shopping on Lee Lane in Covington.*
Courtesy Louisiana Office of Tourism

**Above:** *Zydeco band performs at Louisiana Folklife Festival in Monroe.*
Courtesy Louisiana Office of Tourism

**Above:** *Stained glass ceiling of the Old State house in Baton Rouge.* Courtesy Louisiana Office of Tourism

**Left:** *Elephants delight children at the Audubon Zoo in New Orleans.* Courtesy Louisiana Office of Tourism

**Right:** *Decorated boats lead the Shrimp and Petroleum Festival in Morgan City.* Courtesy Louisiana Office of Tourism

**Above:** *Dr. Hazel Barton rappels down from a balcony hovering over elementary students from Pineville at Sci-Port Discovery Center.* Courtesy The Times archives

**Left:** *Peeling crawfish at the Crawfish Festival in Breaux Bridge.* Courtesy Louisiana Office of Tourism

**Right:** *Children enjoying watermelon at the Watermelon Festival in Ruston.* Courtesy Louisiana Office of Tourism

**Below:** *The giant omelette is mixed during the Giant Omelette Festival in Abbeville.* Courtesy Louisiana Office of Tourism

**Above:** *Hannah and her mom, Rachael, wait for "dad" Staff Sgt. Richard to arrive at Barksdale Air Force Base as more than 2000 troops returned from overseas in May 2002.* Courtesy The Times archives

**Above, left:** *1st Lt. Kevin (rt) kisses his wife, Gina, after arriving at Barksdale Air Force Base.* Courtesy The Times archives

**Above:** *Sunset on the Mississipi at the Interstate 10 Bridge, Baton Rouge.* Courtesy Louisiana Office of Tourism

**Right:** *Tarby Tarver makes a Raku Fired pot at the Festivals Acadiens in Lafayette.* Courtesy The Advertiser archives

*Louisiana Purchase: A Pictorial Retrospective Celebrating Louisiana*